More
Hidden Walks
in the Bay Area

More
HIDDEN WALKS
in the
BAY AREA

Pathways, Essays, and Yesterdays

By
Stephen Altschuler

Western Tanager Press
Santa Cruz

Copyright © 1991 by Stephen Altschuler

"Falling" originally appeared as "Falling Free" in the *San Francisco Chronicle*, March 10, 1991. "Coyote" originally appeared as "The Call of the Coyote" in the *East Bay Express*, January 4, 1991.

Cover design by Lynn Piquett
Text design by Michael S. Gant
All photographs by the author unless otherwise credited
Maps by Andy Huber
Typography by TypaGraphix

ISBN: 0-934136-48-3

Library of Congress Card Catalog Number: 91-65274

Printed in the United States on 80 percent recycled paper

Western Tanager Press
1111 Pacific Avenue
Santa Cruz, CA 95060

This book is dedicated to the memory of Henry David Thoreau, a great walker — and thinker — with whom I feel a close affinity. In his essay *Walking*, he wrote, "My vicinity affords many good walks; and though for so many years I have walked almost every day, and sometimes for several days together, I have not yet exhausted them. An absolutely new prospect is a great happiness, and I can still get this any afternoon."

Exactly my sentiments about the Bay Area.

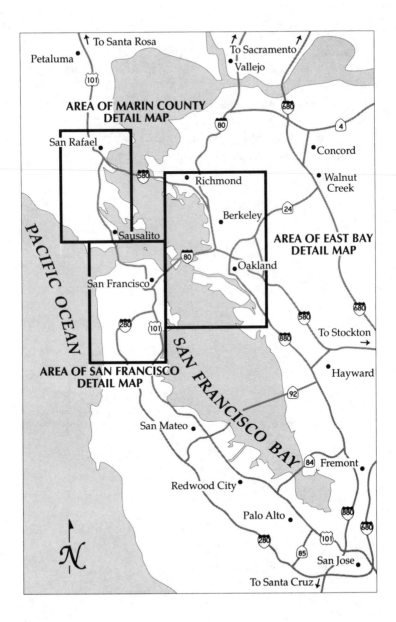

Table of Contents

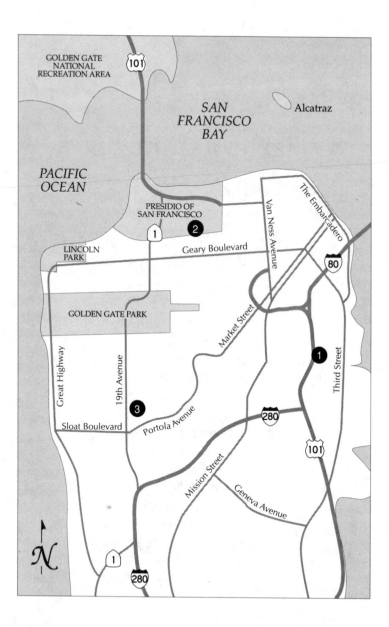

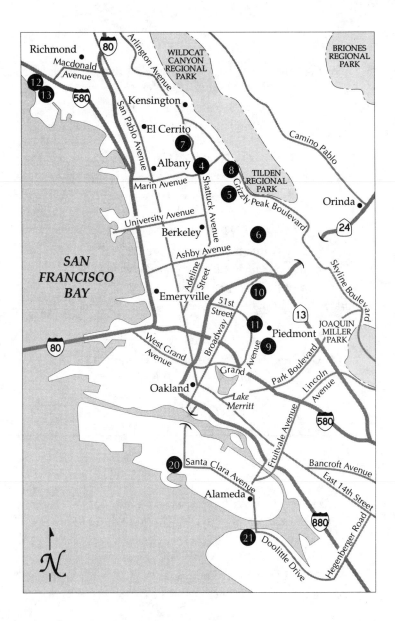

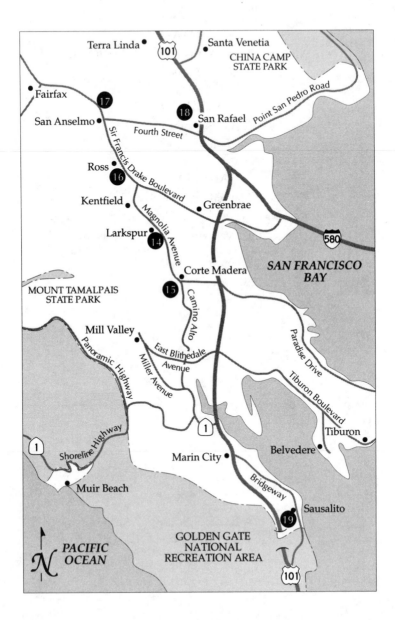

Acknowledgements

I'd like to thank the following people for their help in bringing this book into being: Hal Morris, Karin Mallory, and Michael Gant at Western Tanager Press; horticultural identification assistance from Carl Gancher, Laura Deome, and John Bryan; Adah Bakalinsky, who shared some gems not covered in her book, *Stairway Walks of San Francisco;* and friends and relatives acknowledged in the first book, with the addition of Jane Brockman and Bob Stoltenberg, as well as all the good folks at Towne House Creative Living Center.

Introduction

When I finished my first book, *Hidden Walks in the Bay Area*, the Loma Prieta earthquake was two months old and I was seriously considering moving to Ashland, Oregon, where the only thing that shook was the Elizabethan stage after a thunderous applause. That, along with exasperating freeway congestion, the high cost of living, and the supposition that I'd probably found every hidden walking lane and trail there was to find in the Bay Area, had me checking Ashland real estate ads.

However, after subsequent walks and conversations with Bay Area locals, it became clear there were still many hidden footpaths out there, prompting more exploration. What followed was a renaissance of rediscovery that quelled my lover's quarrel with the Bay Area. I fell in love all over again with its hills, dales, waterways, and neighborhoods, and decided to stay and write another book.

The Point Richmond walks first renewed that enthusiasm for this area. Who would have imagined it? Nestled behind grids of railroad tracks and oil storage tanks, the town had been a blur on the way to Marin. But that first climb up Nicholl Nob, seeing the bay—all of the bay—I felt as the Spaniard Sargento Ortega, of the Portola Expedition, must have felt in 1769 when he became the first European to sight the bay, after local Indians led him and his troops to Sweeney Ridge to the south.

Despite some rough idling and faulty starts, I was grateful life had led me to this point in time and place. As a walker, there was a sense of fulfillment as well, knowing there were very few other places in the world like this—places where the urban and the natural were so near, indeed where some of the residential urban areas couldn't be separated from the natural. The landscape, apart from the clogged freeways, was nurturing. And standing there on Nicholl Nob, seemingly square in the middle of it all, I felt embraced.

A short time later, an architect friend introduced me to the work of J. B. Jackson, founder of the journal *Landscape,* and a retired UC Berkeley professor who taught classes on the American landscape. Jackson's seminal ideas helped slice through some final resistances to staying here, for he scanned the landscape with a broad eye, emphasizing that all aspects of it, even roads and freeways, needed not so much to be judged but understood in studying the evolution of the physical community. From that base of understanding, reasoned change could happen.

However, a background in psychology told me Jackson was not addressing another aspect of the American landscape—an inner landscape of individual minds that either reacts to or causes the changes in the outer landscape. With that awareness, I began to see my essays as an examination of my own inner landscape and how it relates to the surrounding environment and ecology. A tree was not just a tree, but was a tree as I related to it in my unique way in a given moment of my life. Spring did not just arrive each year, but arrived in the context of all the other springs in this lifetime, and what was happening in my life during that particular spring.

My inner landscape, then, defined the depth, breadth, and mood of my perception of the outer. And by writing about those perceptions, I was opening the way to a closer connection to everything in that landscape. This felt like a more solid base to stand on in trying to change values that have led us to the edge of irreversible damage.

To look at the Bay Area from some high place evokes feelings—feelings of excitement from the interplay of water, land, and light; feelings of disgust at the sight of yellow air, heavy with the miasma of all we consume; feelings of anger at the greed that has shrunk the bay and polluted its water; feelings of love at seeing deer, coyotes, foxes, songbirds, hawks, and owls so close to where we've settled. By exploring such feelings, values can arise, and from those values, action.

The environmentally sensitive lanes, steps, paths, and houses built in late-nineteenth- and early-twentieth-century northern California, were reflections of the values of architects and residents who considered themselves in relation to their environment. So, in the Victorian era, when the majority were trying to separate themselves from nature, the women of Berkeley's Hillside Club said, "Bend the roads! Save the trees!" and those of Mill Valley's Outdoor Art Club resisted even the coming of electricity. They were speaking from a truth hammered into shape on their inner anvil of values—from a sense of what was right, arising from feelings of connection with their outer landscape. From that base of inner understanding, they prevailed and influenced the opinions of the majority.

That same perspective is needed today. These environmental pioneers were acting not from a conceptual ivory tower but from an inner experience they trusted. They understood that change starts from a place within—a place that knows what it values and is willing to risk expressing those values. What we see today in some of the neighborhoods covered in this book are those inner voices manifested.

As the twentieth century progressed, however, other less sensitive voices were speaking and molding the landscape to their values. The automobile and all its ancillary services revolutionized the land. But it wasn't just the automobile: it was the addicted mind set, intoxicated with the convenience of it all, that developed with it. So, eventually, the way neighborhoods were laid out, or houses built, had more to do with where to store and drive cars than with maintaining inner and outer harmony with the environment. In fact inner harmony became equated with whether one's car would start in the morning, and whether the commuting traffic flow would be forgiving that day.

So, despite a Second Bay Tradition style of architecture re-emphasizing environmental harmony and simple lines led by William Wurster in the thirties, one-, two-, and three-car garages were soon waved up from bullpen backyards to an honored mound, next to the front lawn, and even connected to the home itself, with its own inside entrance to the inner sanctum. It was obvious where the priorities were as citizens contracted with the internal-combustion engine, failing to read the fine print which demanded their souls.

The subsequent living areas that arose from this not only did little to mollify the increasing stresses of twentieth-century living, they added to it. Unlike the soothing gardens of North Berkeley, the hidden paths and creeks of Mill Valley, and the high parks and landscaped lanes of Potrero Hill, newer sections had only patch-of-crabgrass front lawns, and a tiny neighborhood mini-playground to mitigate the whir of refrigerators and the hum of toaster, and eventually microwave, ovens.

We've even gotten to the point where many late-twentieth-century people wonder why nature and wildlife are important — guided by the misguided comments of recent U.S. presidents and Department of Interior secretaries — and contemplate their eradication for the sake of convenience and profit. So, wetlands continue to be filled, rain forests denuded, ancient redwoods felled, and high-grass prairies sold to the highest bidder. In local communities, old trees are cut down for better views, power lines are routed through regional parks, and mountain lions are pushed farther into oblivion, not by the gun, but by the advent of the backyard in hitherto wild habitat.

My intention in this book, and in the first one, in addition to providing walking enjoyment, is to encourage environmental awareness on a small level that will eventually translate to a wider one. My intention is to stimulate a consideration of values that will, I hope, lead to a harmonizing of people's needs with those of trees, plants, animals, air, creeks, rocks, and the soil — the earth — itself.

In that sense, the sensitive landscaping of a hillside house lot, creating a pleasing interplay between the natural and the designed, builds a bridge between us and our wild heritage. In that sense, the creative pruning of an old Bishop pine to let light and a view in, instead of hacking it down and ripping out its stump, adds grace and comfort for all who pass by on a flatland street. In that sense, the restoration of a wild creek through a business development or housing site or park makes the landscape that much more organic, including the realm of sound, which can help settle the frazzled nerves of a financial district wizard who walks by on her way home from work.

These are small acts of modifying the outer landscape, arising from an attention to the needs of the inner — needs that have little to do with commerce, profit, or spreadsheets. An outer landscape in tune with the natural order will help keep our inner world poised and better able to respond to the excesses that have already been wrought, as well as prevent further abuses.

Walking these pathways, stairways, and trails may not solve the problems of living. But it will enrich your life and perhaps bring moments of peace and joy. Reflecting on the history of a neighborhood or tree species might not make you an expert on your community's cultural or natural origin. But it will heighten your sense of community, and help make that community more harmonious with its natural background or setting. And reading these essays may not increase your understanding of the world, or your life. But it will remind you of simple things easily forgotten in the din of the day, and in doing so make the ground of your inner landscape more fertile, and the experience of your outer landscape more alive. In this way, perhaps the negative excesses on our planet will be diminished, and the positive wee-small voices of reasoned sensitivity strengthened. At least, that's my hope.

Enjoy the miracle of walking on Earth!

San Francisco

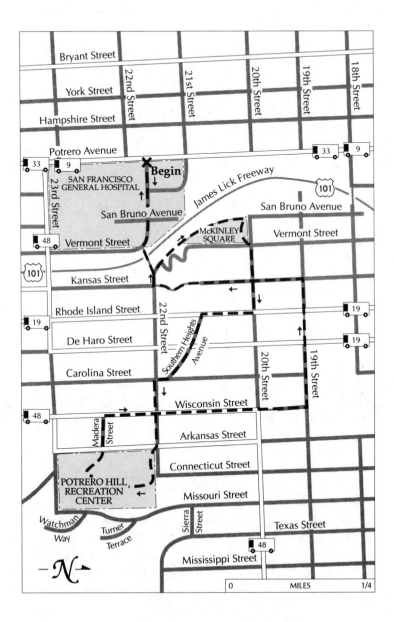

1
Potrero Hill & Views

Terrain: *easy to steep; developed stairways, undeveloped pathways*
Bus Line: *9 San Bruno*
Parks: *Potrero Hill Recreation Center, Espirit Park*
Shops: *Mission district along and around Mission Street, Noe Valley along 24th Street as far as Castro Street*
Distance: *3 miles*
Directions: *From 101 South, take Vermont Street exit to Potrero Avenue to 22nd Street. From 101 North, take Mission Street exit to Mission, then left on 24th to Potrero, and left to 22nd.*

Potrero Hill's recorded history started with the Spanish grazing their cattle there (*potrero* means corral or pasture in Spanish). Ownership of the land was unclear, even after the Mexican government gave the land to the sons of Alcalde Francisco de Haro, San Francisco's first mayor (*alcalde* is the title equivalent to mayor). The transfer was disputed for years, and after the gold rush, squatters began to settle on the hill, taking advantage of all the jobs the gold rush created. Soon, factories followed and ethnic working people from Europe, such as the Irish, Scots, Russians, as well as Yugoslavs and Greeks, flocked to the area, each with their own enclave.

The 1906 earthquake brought more San Franciscans to the area because the hill was relatively unscathed. People carrying babies and bird cages fled their burning homes south of Market to the safer high ground of Potrero Hill, and they were welcomed with open arms and a community spirit that helped them build, first a camp and community, then small houses, some of which are still standing.

This walk explores the hill and features a historic hospital, a street with more curve than the famous Lombard Street, a Julia Morgan–designed community center near the top, and enough hidden steps, lanes, and paths to satisfy the most inveterate trekker of hidden Bay Area urban trails.

The walk starts on Potrero Avenue at 22nd Street, next to San Francisco General Hospital, built on this site in 1872, and the city's first hospital, dating back to 1854. The original wooden buildings are gone, and the brick structure you're seeing was built in 1915. Walk toward the freeway, crossing San Bruno and passing the new AIDS research center as the street bends right. As it does bend, and opposite the parking garage entrance to the center, see the walkway on the left and cross the James Lick Freeway, first admiring the acacia trees that somehow manage to thrive despite the air pollution, then enjoying the dizzying traffic flow, thankful you're not in it.

On the other side is the intersection of Kansas and 22nd streets, with Vermont Street sharply to the left. Take Vermont, past #964, a quaint, tucked-away older cottage, and bear left where the street begins to ascend toward a stairway. You could climb that stairway, but a more interesting and scenic climb would be to mount the steps and trail to the left of the pine tree median strip and the high graffiti-covered wall. This begins the curviest street in San Francisco (according to the city Maps and Survey Department, its degree of curve is more than that of tourist-laden Lombard Street), which you can see as you climb. At one time, the city actually allowed two-way traffic on Vermont, but wisdom prevailed and it was changed to one-way.

At the first landing, see views of Twin Peaks and Sutro Tower beyond and the colorful Mission district below, as steps give way to a dirt path branching to the left. With cypress trees to the right and eucalyptus to the left, the path levels and exits near 20th and Vermont, just to the right of the Potrero Hill Community Garden, a neat and proud effort that deserves a closer look. Its sign concludes with "PLEASE ENJOY OUR GARDEN AND RESPECT our efforts and success. A stolen tomato or eggplant could be <u>so</u> disheartening to anyone." It's a joyful place, and there are more Potrero joys ahead.

Now the city skyline and bay appear—perhaps one of the finest views of one of the most scenic urban areas in the world. Continue up the concrete and wood steps into McKinley Square Park, with wood-crafted sliding boards, play bridges, swings, benches, a sandbox, and a lawn area. Go past the swings to the wide steps at the entrance straight ahead down to the intersection of Vermont and 20th. Stay on 20th to Rhode Island, where brown-shingled apartments are on opposite corners, and go right, passing the Victorian cottage at #830 and a small neighborhood grocery store (a dying breed that I hope will still be there when, and after, this book is published).

At Southern Heights, cross Rhode Island to the left, with views of the hills south of the city, soon reaching a small, tastefully landscaped park at De Haro. Within its stone border are black pine, pyracantha, alyssum, lavender, a young pepper tree, and a wooden semicircular bench, the shape of which will get you talking to a local resident in no time if one joins you for a rest. (By the way, one helpful hint that the author did not heed during an outing here: stay on the organized paths and watch where you place your feet, since the park is sometimes used by dog walkers.)

Across De Haro (named for San Francisco's first *alcalde* or mayor, Francisco de Haro, elected in 1834), on the same side of the street, is the Potrero Hill Neighborhood House, known locally as the Nabe. The simple brown-shingled building was designed by Julia Morgan in 1908, in keeping with the needs of a small community, but wasn't built until 1922. It was given landmark status in 1977 and has remained a continuous hub of community activities. It's open to the general public, so go in and inspect the Julia Morgan interior details.

Past the house, on Southern Heights, see the sweep of the Bay Bridge and a private playground to the left, belonging to a preschool. The street then merges with Carolina Street, which soon meets 22nd Street. Descend left here to Wisconsin, cross 22nd, then use the Wisconsin crosswalk to reach the steps to the right of the median strip and the left of the brown-shingled house at #801. For San Francisco, the grade is gentle, and bay views widen down to Arkansas.

Straight ahead is an undeveloped section of the Potrero Hill Recreation Center. Enter on the dirt path next to a metal pole and walk a short way to Connecticut and 22nd. Pick up the asphalt path to the right, and just before the small playground, rise on a rough dirt trail to the right, and up to the tennis courts. At the level of the courts, see and take a path straight ahead that rises behind a cyclone fence, winding above the courts. Keep bearing left, with the city skyline filling the view. Jag to the left at the top and out the gate of the recreation center to Arkansas.

Opposite the entrance to the center, cross to Madera and climb the short stretch to Wisconsin, turning right and admiring the shingled house and fence of #893, with a brick courtyard of potted flowers and an old graceful pepper tree. At streetside are sycamore and bottle brush, and on the corner of 22nd, old Number 48 fire station, which has been serving the area since 1915.

Continuing down Wisconsin, see the unusual wood sculpture at #760 and several late Victorians, some with scalloped shingles. At #692, there's a California buckeye behind a bamboo fence and rustic gate. And, of course, the views here of the city and bay are legendary.

At 20th, turn left and cross Carolina, but before climbing 20th, just before a handsome black pine, go right at the crosswalk and take the steps with railing next to a large ivy-covered, brown-shingled apartment house (the steps are just to the left of a black-and-white guard rail). Descend between a miniforest and the terraced house. At the bottom, Carolina continues to 19th, with the Potrero Hill Middle School just ahead and the public Jackson Playground just beyond the school.

Turn left and climb 19th on the kind of humbling hill San Francisco is known for. As you walk past the pampas grass hillside on the school grounds, look back and see pigeons roosting on eaves over the school windows. At the top is De Haro Street and a gabled Victorian and garden.

Between that country-in-the-city estate and the brown-shingled house next to it on the left, find a dirt pathway, next to the phone pole and bordered by small rocks and flowers on either side. Wind your way up this delicate gem of a hidden, almost magical path to Rhode Island and 19th. Cross and stay on 19th, with its row of simple cottages on the right and the yucca trees on the corner, to Kansas, where you go left to more great views.

Ascend Kansas, cross 20th, and continue on this "Not a Through Street" (for cars). Walkers can go to the end, past the rocky hillside, and down the asphalt driveway/right-of-way, past neat cottages, to the stone-embanked, cyclone fence–encased steps straight ahead. These wind down, on broken stone and concrete, under eucalyptus and pittosporum, to another right-of-way next to a sprawling pepper tree. Bear left, past an Italianate apartment house, down toward the Monterey pine and Kansas and 22nd.

Cross, and return to the right on the same freeway pedestrian overpass to Sheedy Street and 22nd Street around the bend to the right. Return to Potrero, or explore the hospital and its grounds if you have time. There are gardens and a courtyard between the gray, main building and the new AIDS research building, a huge decorative fountain near the emergency room parking lot, and a historical photo display, commemorating 105 years of cooperation between the city and the hospital, in the second floor cafeteria in the main building. A little education mixed with recreation and exercise is often a good thing.

Julia Morgan: Architect

S he was a most unusual woman for her day. Born in San Francisco on January 20, 1872, and raised in Oakland, she decided early to follow in her cousin's footsteps and become an architect, which at the time was a virtually unheard of aspiration for a woman. Yet Julia Morgan was gifted in mathematics and, with great determination, eventually became the first woman to graduate from UC Berkeley's Engineering school. Still, architecture was another matter. There were no architecture schools in California at the time, and the most prestigious school, L'Ecole des Beaux-Arts, in Paris, had never accepted women, or even allowed them to take the stiff entrance examination.

But one of her teachers at Berkeley, Bernard Maybeck, encouraged her to try to gain admittance, and employed Morgan after her graduation from Berkeley in 1894. He even went further and recommended her to the Ecole, and this convinced her family to send her to Paris to study for the entrance exam.

As the story goes, when Morgan was ready, she put up her hair, posed as a man, passed the exam with such high marks that the Ecole couldn't refuse her even when they found out her gender. Maybeck's reference, of course, helped, too, and the regents were not disappointed. She was an excellent student and received certification in 1902.

With her Beaux-Arts credentials, she was in demand, and first worked for John Galen Howard, helping to design the UC campus at Berkeley. Morgan soon developed a reputation for excellence and attention to detail, and after working on teams developing the Hearst Mining Building and the Greek Theatre, she set off on her own, building a business, with the aid of sorority contacts, despite much discrimination against women in this profession. In fact, some firms did not want architectural drawings signed by women for fear their male clients would object; and one of Morgan's colleagues, Charlotte Mesic, changed her name to C. Julian Mesic to avoid such bias. Even Morgan, under pressure from one of her long time male draftsmen, took an expedient course once in rejecting the application of a woman architect, since it would have created a majority of women on her staff, which, she felt, would have adversely affected her business.

So business did come in — a great deal of it from women clients. There were the Bell Tower and Library at the all-woman Mills College in Oakland between 1903 and 1906, the restructuring of the Fairmont Hotel in San Francisco after the 1906 earthquake, Young Women's Christian Association (YWCA) buildings in Oakland and San Jose, and the well-known Asilomar in Pacific Grove — originally the YWCA's conference center. It was eventually awarded state monument status. She also designed St. John's Presbyterian Church (now the Julia Morgan Theater) in Berkeley, as well as many architecturally important houses in Vallejo, Woodside, San Rafael, Piedmont, Berkeley, and Mt. Shasta (including a collaboration with Maybeck on the Hearsts' fabulous Gothic retreat called Wyntoon on the McCloud River).

She successfully combined Beaux-Arts classicism with the Northern California First Bay Tradition vernacular, but the structure she is most famous for is Hearst Castle in San Simeon, as the lines today waiting to see it will attest. She had met the Hearst family early on, and their commissions greatly enhanced her career. Though the castle looks like it was built for royalty, Morgan considered nature in the design. The main building is on a hillside, surrounded by three cottages and a pool, which in turn surround a garden. The cottages were situated and named according to their relation to nature: the Casa del Mar (sea), the Casa del Sol (sun), and the Casa del Monte (mountain). And like her and Maybeck's work in hilly areas throughout the Bay Area, everything follows the contours of the hillside.

She was more conservative in nature and practice than her mentor, Maybeck, but she was a master at figuring out design problems in relation to the living needs of her clients, and balancing the dictates of the landscape as well. When one client asked her what color to paint his home's interior, she advised him to check the bark and leaves of nearby eucalyptus trees and match it to that.

Julia Morgan left a rich architectural legacy during her 40 years of practice. By the time she retired in 1951, she received emeritus status in the American Institute of Architects, having designed more than 800 homes and other buildings, many of which still stand.

There's been a revival of interest in Morgan's work in the late twentieth century, due to her skillful blending of the functional and the aesthetic—recognition she did not foresee. When she closed her San Francisco office, she burned most of her files and blueprints, assuming that her clients had their own copies and that no one else would be interested in them. She did keep all her correspondence with the Hearst family, however.

Unfortunately, Julia Morgan's final years were sad and tragic, steeped in loneliness and despair. Her work was her life, never having married or had children, so when her career wound down, she began to lose her mental and physical capacities. On her last overseas trip, by freighter to Spain and Portugal in 1947, she absentmindedly failed to return to the ship at the scheduled time and was not permitted ashore at the next port. And later, during an excursion to some old Oakland haunts, she was mugged and had to be hospitalized. These events drove home to her the truth that her faculties were failing, a fact she had enormous difficulty accepting after such a vibrant and creative career. With her favorite brother dead and the rest of her family scattered about the country and busy with their own lives and careers, Morgan hired a nurse/caretaker and retreated to her bedroom, from which she never emerged for the last four years of her life. Ignored by former close associates and, except for a sister, by the rest of her family, Morgan died on February 2, 1957. She was 85.

The next day, the *San Francisco Chronicle*, owned by her most valued client, the Hearst family, acknowledged her contributions to architecture, emphasizing the vocational and scholarship assistance she extended to other women trying to enter this field. In 1988, a major book appeared — the first — about Julia Morgan's life and work (see Supplemental Reading).

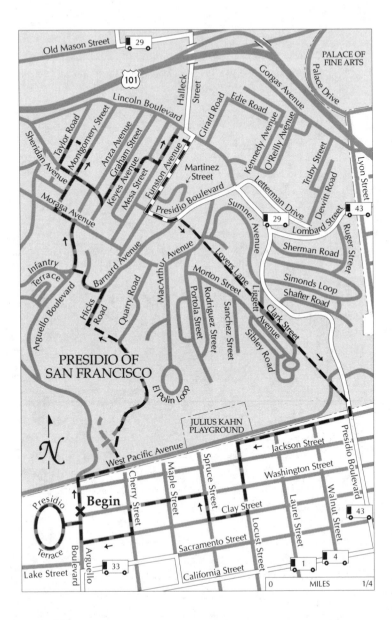

2
Presidio Lowlands & Heights

Terrain: *easy to moderate; improved lanes, unimproved footpaths and trails*
Bus Lines: *33, 1, 4*
Parks: *Golden Gate National Recreation Area, Fort Mason, Crissy Field, Palace of Fine Arts/Exploratorium, Mountain Lake, Julius Kahn Playground*
Shops: *Sacramento Street, Marina District*
Distance: *4.5 miles*
Directions: *From 101 North, take Fell Street to Masonic. Follow to Presidio Boulevard, go left on California, then right on Arguello to Washington.*

This walk may cover the best of all possible urban worlds: the historic, the residential, and the natural. The Presidio of San Francisco is a 1,400-acre tract that has been a military base since 1776. Within its boundaries are forests, beaches, cliffs overlooking the ocean, historic buildings, bay and city views, and the last free-flowing creek in San Francisco. Just to the south is Presidio Heights, an exclusive residential area that includes houses by Maybeck, Morgan, and Wurster. Not all of it will be included, but your appetite will be whetted to explore further.

Start on Arguello Boulevard, at Washington Street, near one of the entrances to the Presidio. Climb past Jackson Street, to the entrance, and pass through the gates, remembering that this is not only part of the Golden Gate Recreation Area, but is also still a U.S. Army base (the base will be phased out over several years, and eventually, the National Park Service will completely control the Presidio), and visitors, though entirely welcome, are subject to search at any time for any reason. Take a sharp right onto West Pacific Avenue, the unsigned road to the right of Arguello. Pick up the dirt trail to the left, next to the No Parking sign and the multitrunk eucalyptus.

After a short distance, just before the trail starts to descend, see another trail, between rows of eucalyptus, to the left, opposite the beige, brick building with five rectangular bay windows. Very shortly, a wider dirt trail crosses this one, which you take to the right. Descend past lacy white pine, cypress, and eucalyptus into part of the Presidio forest, which resulted from the planting, in 1883, of over 400,000 trees — an effort initiated by U.S. Army Corps of Engineers Major W. A. Jones, who wanted to "crown the ridges, border the boundary fences, and cover the areas of sand and marsh waste with a forest." The drought has definitely taken its toll, but in the Presidio's Mediterranean climate, most trees have thrived (a new beetle from Australia, however, is threatening the eucalyptus trees, prompting grounds personnel to consider introducing more native, disease- and drought-resistant tree species).

This is actually called Quarry Road, winding past an open hillside on the left and a picnic area below to where the road is paved and a group of houses begins. To the right of the first house (#820D), next to a utility pole, find a concrete path, with a couple of pavement squares decorated with rope impressions, and follow it down steps to an athletic field. Go right, around the field, to a parking lot and exit to the right on Hicks Road, which leads to Bernard Avenue outside the parking lot.

Bear left on wooded Bernard, which soon returns to a dirt surface, and winds to the right. At an opening and intersection of another dirt trail, turn sharply left up toward the palm tree and brick house on the rise straight ahead. Passing cypress groves, come to Arguello (which is what you would've stayed on if you'd driven from the entrance) and Infantry Terrace. Cross and go right on this cypress-lined sidewalk toward limited bay views, past the mission-style post library on the left, down to Moraga Avenue and a Phoenix palm and Italian stone pines. Turn left, crossing the exit to the post childcare center, then a right on Montgomery Street at the crosswalk.

This is the start of the historic main post of the Presidio, and site of the original Spanish garrison (*presidio* means garrison). The only thing that remains of the original buildings is part of an adobe wall, which is preserved and accessible to the public, in the Officers Club back on Moraga, adjacent to the library. Walk down Montgomery past these brick buildings, originally used as enlisted men's barracks during the Indian Wars. The large parking lot was the main parade ground when the Presidio was an embarkation point for troops going to war. Proceeding under mature acacias (unfortunately, these trees will be removed over the next couple of years due to drought-induced disease) and past young liquidamber trees (planted to gradually replace the acacia), the old fenced eucalyptus in the parking lot (this is the U.S. Centennial tree, planted in 1876), and the smaller, fenced Monterey cypress (the Bicentennial tree, planted in 1976), go left after the third building, on a path beside the black iron railing, to see a unique view of the Golden Gate Bridge through the grove of cypress trees.

Turn left on Taylor to see what these historic barracks look like from the rear, and see more handsome brick houses to the right. Continue toward the wood frame house, with two Phoenix palms, to Sheridan Avenue, where you turn left. Cross Montgomery, pass Arguello and the Officers Club, then Anza Avenue, coming to Graham Street. Go left, admiring the yucca trees and getting a close look at the Walker Bull Dog tank on display to the left, named for Lt. Walton "Bulldog" Walker, who, we assume, either designed the "highly mobile 25-ton fighting unit" or looked like one.

Now cross Owen Street and go right at the crosswalk to the paved path to Keyes Avenue, next to the Sixth Army Headquarters building. Take the sidewalk to the left, next to the building, to Canby Street, where a right brings you to a small street with no name. Turn left toward the Army missile display, then right at the wooden signs marked "Greely St." and "34th Ave." This building is the Presidio Army Museum, and the small cottages to the left are the only structures that remain of refugee housing after the 1906 earthquake. One has authentic furnishings, and the other a photo history of the relief effort in the nearby Richmond district after the big quake and fire.

Continue around the building, past the large cannon and, if you have time, tour the museum, which originally was a Civil War post hospital, built in 1864. The museum could keep you occupied for a long time, with its historic photos, dioramas, artifacts, period clothing, and fascinating, and perhaps little-known, history, not only of the military but also of early San Francisco. The history of the Presidio and the city are closely woven together.

When you've had your fill, take the steps in front of the museum down to Funston Avenue. Turn right, walking on this quiet street of older brick houses, pines, palms, cypresses, and a small playground to the left. Pass Martinez Street, then go left at Presidio Boulevard, with yucca trees and the Army's version of the Victorian house.

Just past Bernard, cross Presidio carefully on the white-lined crosswalk, picking up an unsigned asphalt footpath, known as Lover's Lane, leading down and crossing an old brick bridge, with equally old eucalyptus trees on the drainage ditch banks. This lane may be one of the oldest in the city because it's part of a Spanish trail that once connected the Presidio with Mission Dolores.

Now cross MacArthur Avenue, staying straight on the now concrete pathway. Ascend gradually beside eucalyptus, cypress, and post housing as the lane becomes all dirt. Cross Liggett Avenue, continuing as the path parallels Clarke Street, with brick homes bordered by mature cypress trees. Clarke soon veers right as you stay straight on Lover's Lane, now broken asphalt and dirt, ascending through the Presidio forest, past the snakelike trunks of leptospermum or tea trees—an Australian native—up to West Pacific Avenue. Cross and continue to the old rusted entrance gates, flanked by two large pines.

Exit to Presidio Boulevard, then turn right at Pacific Avenue and into an entirely different world of individualized elegance—the world of Presidio Heights. There are stylish brown-shingled houses, with decorative windows and doors and London plane trees that make the street seem like a page out of London, England. Pass Walnut Street, seeing the extensive cypress forest to the right, along with Golden Gate Bridge views, as Pacific narrows. Of architectural note is a sprawling, though fairly simple, house at #3377, designed by Julia Morgan in 1908. Here, too, is the Julius Kahn Public Playground to the right, a nice diversion if you have kids along.

Cross Laurel Street, then go left at Locust Street, where you can view the fabulous Roos House on the northwest corner at Jackson Street. The impressive house, which is still owned by the Roos family, was designed by Bernard Maybeck in 1909, his own version of the English Tudor style on a hillside lot.

When you're through marveling at the house—I hope Mrs. Roos is used to this sort of thing—continue up Locust past houses of quarry stone, brick, and white shingles, cross Washington Street, and turn right on Clay Street, which is just about as high as Presidio Heights gets. Across the street on the southwest corner, at #301, is an unassuming, irregularly shingled, board-and-batten house designed by William Wurster in 1954—an example of the Second Bay Tradition of architecture he spearheaded in the thirties and forties. And farther down as you walk on Clay is an earlier Wurster at #3655, built in 1942, and a simple Second Bay Tradition answer to the classic pomp and elegance that surround it. Its windows are functional, its roof low-pitched, and, perhaps in response to the increasing number of automobiles at the time, the garage is attached to the house and faces the street. Previously, garages were often hidden from view and not part of the street-front facade as they are in modern designs today. By the way, Wurster's style led to the California ranch house, which eventually spread throughout the country.

Now go right at Spruce Street to Washington, with bay views and more interesting architecture. On the northeast corner is #3700, designed by the highly influential architect Joseph Esherick in 1952—a blend of informal barn siding and many windows, and more formal iron work and entry way. And by way of contrast, as you continue on Washington, just past Maple Street, at #3800, is the baronial Koshland Mansion, built in 1902, where one expects Louis XVI to emerge any moment. In a play on opposites, note the TV satellite dish on the roof.

A bit farther is another architectural contrast: the Presidio Hill School, formerly called the Presidio Open Air School, at #3839. It was built in 1918, and its board-and-batten siding and shuttered windows make it look like a country schoolhouse. At Cherry Street, turn left, on a level grade, past a variety of brown-shingled, Victorian, and modern houses to a right on Clay.

Descend past brick and brown-shingled houses to views of an unusual building typed as Arabo-Byzantine: Temple Emanu-El, a synagogue designed, in part, by Bernard Maybeck in 1926. Across Arguello, you can peek into the courtyard and enjoy some of the details of design, or take a closer look as you check with the office about tours of the synagogue.

The walk has now looped back to the beginning, but it's not quite over. Straight ahead is the entrance to Presidio Terrace, "a remarkable collection of pretentious piles," according to *The Guide to Architecture in San Francisco and Northern California*, "the most remarkable being No. 30, an immense Hansel and Gretel cottage by MacDonald & Applegarth, 1909." In fact, that particular house, just to the left of the entrance gate, is home, as of this writing, to Dianne Feinstein, former mayor of the city and, in 1990, an unsuccessful candidate for governor. And another (#34, also designed by Golden Gate Park's Legion of Honor architect George Applegarth in 1909) is home to the Alioto family — Joseph Alioto being a former mayor as well. It's a fun walk around the circle, reviewing the manifestations of wealth and status, along with seeing the synagogue from a different angle. Arguello is the line that separates Presidio Heights and the Richmond District, so you are now officially in the latter.

The walk concludes on Arguello and Washington, although you might wish to explore spring-fed Mountain Lake and its pleasant park several blocks to the west on Lake Street, and wild Lobos Creek, the city's last remaining open creek, which supplies the Presidio with all its water needs from an underground aquifer, farther west within the Presidio boundary.

Mud Walking

I have a long and storied relationship with mud. It goes back to early spring days in New England, where, on some forest roads in New Hampshire, the only alternative to the muddy road was the forest thicket. There, it was called spring, which I suppose was an attempt to lighten the burden of mud. Here, in California, it's called winter or the rainy season, which is more in tune with the true nature of mud. There, mud was a survival thing—newly transplanted emigres from Boston would suddenly disappear, only to reappear on a hot sticky summer day, wandering dazed down a dusty country road. Here, mud is a more forgiving medium, since most people don't have to go through it to get home, so they walk around it, or don't walk at all. In California, there are many choices. In New Hampshire, there was pretty much only one.

But I seek out mud here. It's harder to find because a lot of walks are way up, then way down, so the rain drains too quickly for good, deep mud to develop. There are trails and undeveloped paths, though, where a rich base of mud has been churned in. It's something we humans have really perfected—the creation of mud. For nature itself doesn't produce high-quality mud. Oh, occasionally a river bed may have some—though too solid, usually—and sometimes a swamp, on its way to meadowhood, may have high mud content. But it's people or the animals most associated with people, like cows, dogs, and horses, that make really good, slimy mud, mixing and churning and stirring, creating ridges and grooves and mini–mud canyons that challenge the best mud walkers around.

In fact, I was glad to see paleontologists corroborate this phenomenon when they found an ancient human footprint on an African tundra, preserved in lava mud, now dried and hardened. Even 10–15,000 years ago we were perfecting our mud-making abilities. I'm sure if there had been a little water on the moon, Neil Armstrong would have walked, jumped, and driven through it, creating "one small step for man" and one giant mud puddle for mankind. I've never seen humans pass up an opportunity to make mud.

Now this is not a criticism of our species, for mud can lead to metaphysical awakenings. It's the instability of it, the uncertainty. Mud actually makes the ground move, and we like our ground to be solid. After all, mud is matter, and matter is supposed to be cohesive, with organized molecules holding it all together in orderly fashion. Walking on mud creates a whole new level of consciousness. No longer can we smugly predict the earth will support us, will stay still, while we move about. Maybe that's why Californians, for the most part, seem to avoid mud. Earthquakes thoroughly satisfy any needs for terrestrial instability.

There is a certain technique to mud walking — one that allows for creativity and relative stability. It involves leaning backward slightly on the heels, keeping the arms buoyant and stretched like a tightrope walker's balancing pole, and fixing the eyes about four feet in front, scanning the frontier of the next step. You enter the mud more with your heart than feet, like a 90-meter ski jumper preparing to fly. Steps are not just steps, but little adventures involving tiny slips and slides. Your internal navigator must make rapid adjustments, but, alas, mud is too changeable, too unpredictable for that gyroscope in the brain.

So, by walking in mud, we are forced to explore our limits. How far out of control will we allow ourselves to become? How close will we risk disaster, and do we somehow crave a crisis? Do we somehow, on some level, want to lose our ground and fall in the mud? Is there a three-year-old in all of us that wants to wallow, that wants to be totally covered in mud? And if there is an inner child in all of us that needs to be healed, as the pop psychologists tell us, wouldn't mud be better, and more fun, therapy than talking to a psychotherapist for x years?

I've never fallen in a good mud puddle, nor have I walked barefoot in one, so I guess my adult is in charge, those same psychologists would tell me. But maybe I've just honed my mud-walking technology too well. I don't think technology was ever meant to get us away from nature, but we just got so good at it that we took a few extra steps and felt like we were beyond nature. At least that was the illusion. As nature has shown us we weren't beyond it, but such lessons apparently require repetition.

I passed one fellow on an Oakland path, however, who was completely covered with mud and, along with his companion, was laughing and carrying on about it. It was a great advertisement for not getting too skilled at mud walking, for I envied the anarchy of the way he looked—totally out of control, yet laughing like a loon. I smiled and made some flip comment, but it was he who was really having fun with life. I was merely an observer looking out from behind my mind.

There wasn't much mud this year (1990), as the drought continued. What little there was deepened my understanding of, and relationship with, mud (along with my love of the word mud, which I've just become aware of using in almost every sentence in this discourse). There's so much more to unlearn, though. Next year, I hope to loosen my technique a bit, perhaps reining in my balance-pole arms, allowing a fall, and lying there laughing. Maybe then, in full embrace, mud and I will marry, and live happily ever insecure.

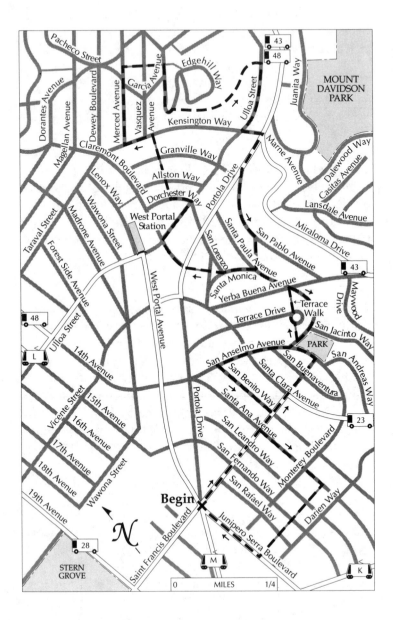

3

St. Francis Wood & Beyond

Terrain: *easy to moderate; improved paths and steps, undeveloped paths and trails*
Bus Lines: *K, L, M streetcars (Muni), 43 Masonic (bus)*
Parks: *Sigmund Stern Recreation Grove, Pine Lake, Harding, San Francisco Zoological Gardens, Mt. Davidson*
Shops: *19th Avenue, Ocean Avenue*
Distance: *4.5 miles*
Directions: *From 101, take 280 toward Daly City. Exit at Monterey Boulevard (or Ocean Avenue) and follow to Junipero Serra. Turn right to St. Francis Boulevard.*

The stylish St. Francis Wood section of San Francisco was the brainchild of innovative Berkeley developer Duncan McDuffie, who set out to break the San Francisco tradition of bunching houses close together. He enlisted the aid of noted architects and planners such as John Galen Howard, Henry Gutterson, and Louis Christian Mullgardt, and entrusted the landscape design to none other than Frederick Law Olmstead, famous for New York's Central Park, Stanford's campus, and Mountain View Cemetery. What resulted was a distinctive, spacious neighborhood, with many original, mature trees, and a tasteful Spanish Colonial Revival architectural style, along with some English, French, and Mediterranean designs.

It was one of the first planned communities of family homes, initiated a few years after the 1906 earthquake. Residents even formed their own improvement association (the St. Francis Homes Association is still very much active), exercising architectural controls, and maintaining common areas through assessment fees. Combined with the great views, stairways, hidden lanes, and forest trails of the more working-class West Portal area, this long walk should season your tastes of exploring San Francisco.

Start at the foot of St. Francis Boulevard, where it intersects with Junipero Serra. It's at the major intersection of Portola Drive and Sloat Boulevard and near a streetcar tunnel that goes all the way to Market Street, opening this area to increased development and interest after it was completed in 1917. The Grecian entrance portals and courtyard were designed by John Galen Howard (who founded the school of architecture at UC Berkeley) in 1912 and accentuated by young Monterey pine trees, which replaced original decorative fountains. Promenade up the broad St. Francis Boulevard (Saint Francis, of course, was the patron saint of San Francisco), seeing variations on the Spanish Colonial theme and admiring the ornate sidewalks, with bricks for borders and diamond accents. Cross a succession of streets, lined with the flowering *Eucalyptus ficifolia* (there are more than 700 varieties of eucalyptus, four of which are represented in St. Francis Wood). First there's San Rafael, noting #100, with wooden porch and characteristic round mission-style mock bell tower, then San Leandro, and Santa Ana, where you reach The Circle, whose center fountain was designed, in 1913, by Henry Gutterson, at that time a close associate of Bernard Maybeck.

Stay on the sidewalk, crossing Santa Ana, and passing the tall Monterey pine to the right. Pass San Benito and the regal palms guarding the entrance to #402. Then cross Santa Clara where a center median strip starts, landscaped with the fragrant pittosporum (try crushing a leaf and using the little-used olfactory sense), and San Buenaventura, with its eugenia trees (adversely affected, like most of the trees in the area, by drought), up to San Anselmo, where St. Francis ends with a concrete terrace, designed again by Gutterson. The adjoining three-acre park, which has no official name, is an Olmstead design and is mostly decorative rather than functional, with mature eucalyptus and Monterey pine. Going left past the park as the street blends into Santa Paula, see the small triangular park with the papery bark melaleuca, another native of the Australasian region.

Straight ahead, across from the triangle, take a path, the unmarked Terrace Walk, between #272 and #199. This leads down, on new redwood steps, to a circle and cul-de-sac, which is the end of Terrace Drive. To the left are tennis courts and a public park, playground, and athletic facilities, maintained by the St. Francis Homes Association, funded by residents to keep public paths, parkways, and parks in good shape (there are seven miles of parkways alone in this 127-acre neighborhood).

Now continue up the Terrace Walk, again on new steps, half way around the circle and storage shed — about the only building around that doesn't comply with architectural standards. The path is left of #165, rising up to Yerba Buena Avenue (*yerba buena* means good herb and was the first name given to San Francisco) and Santa Paula. To the left of the path is a handsome brick and shingle English-style house with diamond windows.

Now cross Yerba Buena, continuing straight on Santa Paula. In a short distance, bear left on Santa Monica, passing acacias and the old weathered English cottage roof of #90. Across the street is a very pleasing quarry stone house with a magnificent cypress on the front lawn. A bit farther, past San Lorenzo, is another median triangle. Opposite #50 Santa Monica, cross to a stepping-stone footpath, traversing the grass (it's highly advisable to stay on this path since people obviously walk their dogs in this common area).

At the end of the path, cross the street and find another short pathway to the left of #37 and the right of a globe-shaped redwood. It's a quiet path leading to very noisy and busy Portola Drive. Cross Portola carefully at the crosswalk to the right to Claremont Boulevard and a section of the city known as West Portal. Walk down to Ulloa and bear right past simple stucco homes, with views of Mt. Davidson to the right. Go left at Dorchester Way, where, partway down, you turn right onto a wide double pathway, with a landscaped median strip. It's to the left of #130 and is unsigned.

Rise gradually, past Allston Way, then Granville Way, to red steps that form a semicircle leading to more steps as the grade steepens. This leads to Kensington Way, at the top, where a left soon brings you to Merced Avenue and a full view of Sutro Tower, near Twin Peaks (Adolph Sutro was a past mayor of San Francisco who once owned most of the land in this part of the city).

Proceed on Merced, crossing first Garcia then Pacheco, where, opposite the small triangle park with decorative urn, you take the wide concrete Grecian-style steps to the right. It's a gentle grade up to Vasquez, which you cross. Then continue up the dirt path, next to the lamppost directly across the street, to Garcia. Cross, using the wooden steps in the middle of the street, then continue to the right, on the sidewalk, straight to Edgehill Way, marked "Not a Through Street" for automobiles. It's also marked as a slide area, which we'll see more evidence of later.

Cross to the sidewalk on the west side, which soon becomes paved with cobblestones, one of the few such sidewalks anywhere in the Bay Area. At one point the sidewalk bows out to a lookout with a black railing—a place to take a break and scan the ocean to the left, Forest Hill straight ahead, and the Golden Gate Bridge to the right.

Now the street horseshoes left, but at the bend, take the driveway/right-of-way to the right, next to the Tudor-style house, named Chateau Folie-a-deux. Pass fir and pine to the end and continue on a pine needle path to the left of the fence and next to the large pine tree. What follows is a forest in the city — land owned by the city — where you stay straight on the trail, past thickets of mixed conifers, across a somewhat open area, to an opening in a cyclone fence. Now climb the small hill to the left, after passing through the fence, coming up to an abandoned tennis court.

The path continues to the right of the court, past a metal post, with fennel and Scotch broom on the right, and views of Mt. Davidson. This exits onto the parking lot of the First Church of the Nazarene, where boulders behind the small fence to the left are examples of how unstable this hillside is. In fact the church had to meet elsewhere between 1985 and 1987 because of the threat of rock slides. High-income houses are planned for this area near the old tennis court, but Pastor Fred Forster assured me the pathway/right-of-way would remain, linking the forest with the church grounds (engineers are stabilizing the hillside in conjunction with the new housing). He also indicated that the public is welcome to pass through church property and extends an invitation to anyone to stop in, say hello, or join the Sunday service.

At the end of the driveway, go right on Ulloa, enjoying ocean views and pueblolike homes. Turn left on Kensington, passing a concrete solution to lawn maintenance, up to Portola. Cross Kensington to the right and walk up the ramp leading to a pedestrian overpass, graced with Italian stone pines and more ocean views. On the other side is Miraloma Drive. Go right along the white wooden fence to steps with railings down to Portola. Bear left a short distance to San Pablo and back into St. Francis Wood, past the entrance pillars.

At Santa Monica, go right, then left on Santa Paula. Continue on this street, crossing Yerba Buena and winding down to San Jacinto. Follow the park to the right, then cross and bear right on San Anselmo, passing London plane trees and Forest Hill views. Pass San Buenaventura, then Santa Clara, noticing there are no overhead utility lines to obstruct views anywhere in St. Francis Wood.

Turn left at San Benito, with eucalyptus lining the street, to the neighborhood's three original sample homes, flanked by tall cypress and Monterey pine. All are Spanish Colonial Revivals, with #44 designed in 1913 by Louis Christian Mullgardt, famous for developing the California bungalow, and #50 and #58 designed in 1914–15 by Henry Gutterson. Subsequent building adhered to this style, with some English and Mediterranean exceptions, as a result of strict architectural controls by the association of residents.

At St. Francis, cross and go right to Santa Ana and The Circle, the center of which is a fountain that normally spouts water. Drought conditions, though, have forced the faucet off. A left on Santa Ana brings you to Monterey with its parkway of black acacia. Cross and continue to a right at a wide double footpath to the left of #240. Walk down the lighted path to ocean views, past connecting driveways, crossing three streets before exiting at a decorative terrace at Junipero Serra. The Ninth Church of Christ, Scientist is on the left, built in a Spanish mission style (notice the Balboa Terrace bus stop in this style, as well).

Walk to the right, toward the tall pine, cross Monterey, and return to St. Francis Boulevard, where this walk of elegance and earthiness began.

From Walking *by Henry David Thoreau*

I have met with but one or two persons in the course of my life who understood the art of Walking, that is, of taking walks, — who had a genius, so to speak, for *sauntering*, which word is beautifully derived "from idle people who roved about the country, in the Middle Ages, and asked charity, under pretense of going *a la Sainte Terre*," to the Holy Land, till the children exclaimed, "There goes a *Sainte-Terrer*," a Saunterer, a Holy-Lander. They who never go to the Holy Land in their walks, as they pretend, are indeed mere idlers and vagabonds; but they who do go there are saunterers in the good sense, such as I mean. Some, however, would derive the word from *sans terre*, without land or a home, which, therefore, in the good sense, will mean, having no particular home, but equally at home everywhere. For this is the secret of successful sauntering. He who sits still in a house all the time may be the greatest vagrant of all; but the saunterer, in the good sense, is no more vagrant than the meandering river, which is all the while sedulously seeking the shortest course to the sea. But I prefer the first, which, indeed, is the most probable derivation. For every walk is a sort of crusade, preached by some Peter the Hermit in us, to go forth and reconquer this Holy Land from the hands of the Infidels.

It is true, we are but faint-hearted crusaders, even the walkers, nowadays, who undertake no persevering, never-ending enterprises. Our expeditions are but tours. and come round again at evening to the old hearth-side from which we set out. Half the walk is but retracing our steps. We should go forth on the shortest walk, perchance, in the spirit of undying adventure, never to return, — prepared to send back our embalmed hearts only as relics to our desolate kingdoms. If you are ready to leave father and mother, and brother and sister, and wife and child and friends, and never see them again, — if you have

paid your debts, and made your will, and settled all your af-
fairs, and are a free man, then you are ready for a walk.

Berkeley

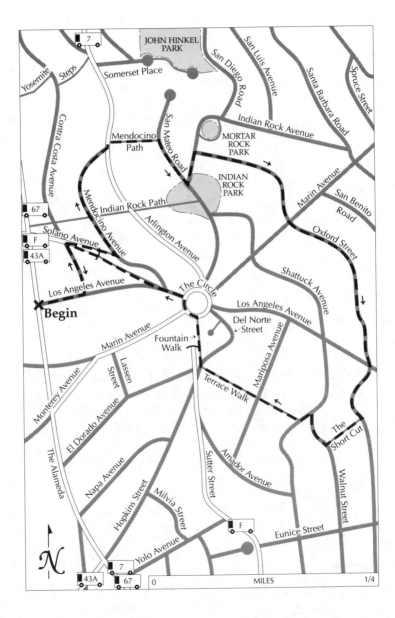

4

Northbrae Ways

Terrain: *easy to moderate; developed paths and steps; undeveloped paths*
Bus Lines: *67, 7*
Parks: *Indian Rock, Mortar Rock, John Hinkel*
Shops: *Solano Avenue*
Distance: *1 mile*
Directions: *From I-80, take Albany exit, go east on Marin Avenue to The Alameda. Turn left to Los Angeles Avenue, just before Solano Avenue.*

As local historian and author Mark Wilson points out, "Berkeley began as dozens of other Bay Area towns had—as a small community of squatters setting up homesteads on a Spanish land grant during the Gold Rush." But with the founding of the university in 1868, and the coming of a railroad line linking Berkeley with Oakland in 1876, Berkeley became a gleam in many a realtor's eyes, and was dubbed "the city of homes," as farms and large estates began to be subdivided and developed into neighborhoods.

Northbrae was such a development, and the finest architects of the day, particularly John Hudson Thomas, contributed in the design of its homes, streets, pathways, parks, schools, and churches. In fact, around the turn of the century, Mason McDuffie Realtors proposed that this area be considered for the state government and even named the surrounding streets for the counties of California in its bid for approval. Obviously they lost out, but they left a section of Berkeley that will win any walker's vote.

The walk starts at The Alameda (which means wide, tree-lined boulevard) and Los Angeles Avenue, next to the Northbrae Community Church. The church was built in 1920 and designed by John Hudson Thomas, who was influenced greatly by a famous contemporary, Frank Lloyd Wright. Thomas was known for his innovative treatment of stucco exteriors and spacious interiors, featuring large bay windows and huge fireplaces. The hearth in the church is 10 feet high. The church and its grounds are open to the public during office hours, and if you're a history buff, ring up the personable minister, Dave Sugarbaker, who may give you a personal tour.

Proceed on Los Angeles, past the church (its gardens have won awards, and there's a hidden waterfall behind the chapel), and go left on Contra Costa Avenue. Carefully cross busy Solano Avenue at the crosswalk and bear right to the path next to the chain-link fence, heading toward the Northbrae Tunnel. This path will take you above the tunnel and passes a huge volcanic boulder, with a cave that would be perfect for temporary shelter in a sudden downpour.

The pathway rises gently to Mendocino Avenue, where you turn left onto this quiet, refined street, highlighted by olive, birch, sycamore, limited bay views, a very English-looking house at #822, and classic John Hudson Thomas houses at #911, built in 1912, and #919, built in 1913. At Arlington Avenue, under a canopy of holly and juniper, cross carefully (this is one of the busiest and speediest streets in North Berkeley) and find the Mendocino Path, signed and just to the right of the crosswalk. This is one of the few fully wheelchair-navigable pathways in the area, as it rises gently through the shadows.

It ends at San Mateo Road, where a right takes you on a level, short walk to Indian Rock Park (Thomas designed #30, known as the Hoyt House, in 1911). Now bear left at Indian Rock Road, unless, of course, you'd first like to climb the steps up ancient Indian Rock and treat yourself to one of the best views in North Berkeley. Pass the stone monument marked "Northbrae" on the corner (these were used by developers to give a sense of identity to the area they were trying to promote) and head up to a right at Oxford, where Thomas designed the 1910 Grigsby House at #915 Indian Rock, with its impressive stone retaining wall and steps, reminiscent of nearby Indian Rock and Mortar Rock parks.

Oxford hugs the hillside and is lined with sycamores and simple houses, until it reaches Marin Avenue, the steepest street in town, originally designed for a cable car but now the bane of brakes, clutches, and upwardly bound pedestrians. Cross carefully and continue under sycamore and privet beside a montage of interesting architectural styles, including the First Bay Tradition with some Grecian features at #918, the stucco masterpieces at #916 and #920, the board-and-batten siding of #976, the Tudor revival at #1014, the brown-shingle with Victorian features at #1019, and #2201, on the corner lot, with its dark redwood boards and windows open to the light and view. It looks like it could be a Maybeck, but it's not.

Now cross Los Angeles Avenue, admiring the brown-shingled Craftsman house at #1106, and look for a footpath to the right, unsigned, just beyond #1128. Descend the gradual grade between privet hedges and the Oxford School. Go right on Walnut Street, graced with birch trees, Japanese maples, and walnut trees. At Shattuck, use the crosswalk and see the sign for the Terrace Walk to the left. Walk down gradually on this path that is suitable for wheelchairs as well, enjoying trumpet vines and toyon. Cross sycamore-lined Mariposa Avenue, where the pathway continues past tucked-away hillside cottages, down to the intersection of Del Norte, Sutter Street, El Dorado, and the Northbrae Tunnel.

Across Del Norte, next to the tunnel, climb the sturdy steps and path of the Fountain Walk, with its iron center railing and Grecian concrete side rails, up and over the tunnel. This brings you to The Circle. (In Boston, these free-for-all anomalies are called rotaries, confronting drivers with the most harrowing of experiences. As for pedestrians, they haven't got a chance there. But in Berkeley, drivers are a tad more polite and will, if they're not recent Eastern transplants, still occasionally stop for a walker entering a crosswalk.) The Circle, by the way, originally had a working decorative fountain in the center—hence the Fountain Walk. However, so many cars smashed into it over the years, as brakes failed coming down Marin, that the fountain was eventually dismantled.

Cross very carefully at the crosswalk to the left, bearing left on Los Angeles. Follow the gravel path above the tunnel, where Mendocino crosses, and continue down to Solano on the other side of the tunnel.

Turn left at Contra Costa, then right at Los Angeles, with the church to your right, and finish at the Northbrae monument pillars where the street joins The Alameda. It would've been a great state capital!

The Dry Season

*T*here is a certain constancy of California weather, between April and September, that is unnerving to a former New Englander. To be able to predict morning fog and afternoon sunshine with near-perfect accuracy seems at variance with basic laws of nature. But contrary to what a New Englander will tell you, those laws of nature were not legislated in New England. The coastal California dry season is a natural body politic all to itself.

Exactly when the dry season starts is a deep mystery. You don't actually notice it until after about a month into it when the front garden seems to be dying. You get so conditioned by the rains that the dryness creeps up on you. It's the magician morning fog that creates the illusion of moisture but only offers sips to the thirsty soil.

There is a lethargy that comes with the dry season. It is a time to relax, rudderless, after a wet and windy winter. It is a time for easy ambling, in shorts and sandals, without a destination or purpose. It is a time to bask. Yet time and the livelihoods that consume it seem particularly cruel during this season. Cool paths await walkers yet are often empty. No one seems to have the time. Everyone is so busy.

The dry season is a quiet, settled time, and its ambience can help nourish quiet within. But you won't notice the quiet in the car or in the supermarket or at the movies. Nor will you notice it while thinking, talking, worrying, planning, lamenting, or mulling. The activity of thought and word have places in our lives, but like the chain-smoker, the chain-talker/thinker never knows any peace, never settles down to the roots. And it's the roots that set the ground, that carry us through the time of scarcity, that grow after the blossom has withered.

The quiet can be found in cool spots under trees in the parks. Trees gather in the breezes, distributing the coolness to anyone who has paused. And the breeze can be a lullaby to those who listen.

Listening to quiet—yes, it takes attention. It takes a moment of removing the knapsack of noise and opening to natural voices. Then the tree breezes speak to internal breezes. Then the slow even-tempo rhythms of the dry season saturate, gently, like the dew. Breath comes more easily, more deeply than before. I settle, relaxed, not knowing exactly where I'm at. Until a voice rattles my reverie.

"Hey, how am I supposed to drive through here with you standing under that tree in the middle of the street, buddy."

"Oh yes. Sorry." (Moral: Listen to the song of dry season silence, but pay attention to where you're standing!)

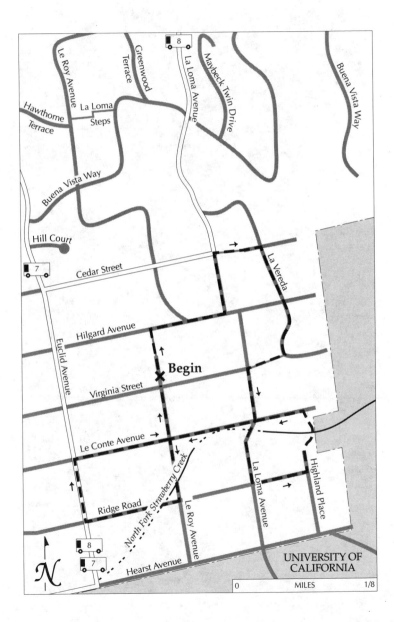

5
Northside Hills, Houses, & a Hidden Canyon

Terrain: *Easy to rough; developed steps, undeveloped paths, rough trail and canyon*
Bus Line: 7
Special Equipment: *Shoes with good traction*
Parks: *Codornices, Rose Garden, UC campus, UC Botanical Garden*
Shops: *Euclid Avenue at Hearst Avenue, downtown Berkeley*
Distance: *2.7 miles*
Directions: *From I-80, take University Avenue exit and head east on University to end. Go left on Oxford Street, then right at Hearst, then left at Euclid a few streets up. A right on Virginia puts you at the walk's start.*

With the university as the hub of their cultural and intellectual life, Berkeley citizens first clustered their houses near it, and this area to the north was one of the earliest. Bernard Maybeck built a prototype of his brown-shingled First Bay Tradition house for his friend and supporter, Charles Keeler, in the area. The Hillside School, one of Berkeley's oldest, is there too, along with the venerable Pacific School of Religion. But in addition to the obvious history, there are also lanes, stairways, trails, and a hidden section of Strawberry Creek that I'm sure Mr. Keeler would've known about, but would probably surprise most present-day locals.

Where Le Roy Avenue ends in a cul-de-sac, just past Virginia Street, climb the cracked concrete steps between flowers, fan palms, live oaks, ivy, and juniper up to Hilgard Avenue. Bear right to where Le Roy continues to the left, cross, and climb a few steps up to the sidewalk, as you stay on Hilgard to the right. Under its oak and ivy canopy, this has the feel of a wooded trail, and at the end a stairway jags to the left, lifting you to La Loma Avenue. Cross carefully, turning left, and ascend this busy street on the sidewalk.

Opposite Cedar Street, at the base of a yield sign, see a rough dirt pathway, which doesn't look like much but is actually a public footpath indicated on local maps. Climb under pine and ivy on footholds and primitive steps near the bottom, skirting a fence farther up and exiting at the end of a cul-de-sac bordered by a concrete post and beam, next to a lemon tree. The right-of-way then leads out to quiet La Vereda, where you go right, descending past Hilgard and bearing left at the fork. At #1680 La Vereda is a 1937 William Wurster design that heralded the back-to-basics Second Bay Tradition style of architecture that thrived through the forties.

Just past the fork, see a wooden bridge where the street bends left to another dead end. Cross the bridge, taking a sharp right down the wooden steps and onto a concrete path and steps to a left at Virginia, before the steps go down farther. The steps spiral down past Tudor and brown-shingles, joining Virginia Street, where you continue down to limited bay and Mt. Tamalpais views. Better than the view is the log and redwood house at the corner of La Loma (#1705 La Loma, but it also faces Virginia), designed in 1907 for William Rees by Bernard Maybeck, with his characteristic Swiss-style balconies, wide eaves, and uneven gabled roofs to accommodate the steep hillside site.

Descend another concrete stairway and go left onto La Loma,

walking along the oak-shaded sidewalk on a street Maybeck and Keeler may have strolled along. Another Maybeck design — the Jockers House — built in 1911, is at #1709. It's stucco, not a favorite material of his before the 1923 fire but chosen here for economy. He still managed to give it a unique signature with roughened and contrasting troweled surfaces. But #1715, the Lillian Bridgeman House and Studio, built and designed by the owner in 1899, with technical assistance from Maybeck, who was also her friend, definitely shows more of his familiar style. Bridgeman was so pleased with the collaboration that she gave up teaching physics, studied architecture, and developed a small, thriving residential practice. The studio behind the main house was her design, built in 1907.

Opposite this house, take the concrete steps down to the street, cross, and continue down on the sidewalk to where Le Conte bends to the right. Cross Le Conte and bear left, staying on La Loma, walking up the sidewalk with a canopy of oak, acacia, plum, yew, and birch.

At Ridge Road, turn left up to the highlands of Highland Place, where you go left. (A right leads to an interesting side excursion, the Nyingma Institute at #1815, a Tibetan Buddhist center, with its array of prayer flags, and bright blues, greens, and aquamarines. Its small bookstore, interior courtyard gardens, and meditation activities are open to all. Just enter the impressive entrance during business hours and introduce yourself. The building, by the way, used to house a men's fraternity, so its consciousness has no doubt been greatly raised by the present Buddhist owners.)

The left on Highland Place — a dead end (whatever happened to signs saying "Dead End" instead of "Not a Through Street"?) — takes you past one of the more famous houses in Berkeley, the Charles Keeler House at #1770 — one of the first designed by his friend, Bernard Maybeck. It and the studio next to it, at #1736, were built in 1895 and represent prime examples (they survived the 1923 fire) of Maybeck's early efforts combining a Gothic style and hillside architecture. The houses have been extensively remodeled, but the setting is the same, set to the rear of a quiet garden filled with jasmine, wisteria, redwood, rhododendron, foxglove, tall palms, and a mossy ancient ground cover. Try imagining Keeler and Maybeck emerging, discussing the latest ideas of the Berkeley Handicraft Guild.

Continue to the end of Highland, where you'll find an opening and a path between the cyclone fence on the left and a guard rail on the right. It starts beyond the several utility company stepping stones and immediately goes right—a rough trail that descends into Woolsey Canyon. The going is a bit difficult and narrow here, so use caution and tree limbs as you climb the short descent into the canyon and a meeting with the North Fork of Strawberry Creek.

At the bottom, bear left, ford the creek (the sagacity of this direction is, of course, dependent on the level of water in the creek), and pick up the trail again on the other side. (There seems to be no poison oak down here, but I can't guarantee it.) Horsetails line the narrow path that leads through a cyclone fence/gate, past a house on the left (you're actually on public utility land here, but please be especially quiet so as not to disturb the residents of this peaceful canyon) to a high step and wooden fence straight ahead.

The fun continues as you mount the high step to the right and push open an old and quite obscure wooden door/gate that leads out to concrete and railroad tie steps down to Le Conte.

Once through the gate, walk straight past La Loma, noticing the simple yet elegant design work of Julia Morgan at #2695, set back from the front grove of relatively young redwood trees. They were likely planted as part of the design when the house was built in 1908.

At Le Roy, bear left, crossing Strawberry Creek again, this time in more genteel fashion, admiring another Maybeck design—

the Maurer Studio — at #1772, which he built in 1907 as a home and gallery for a portrait photographer. The large window and Corinthian column in the front were part of the gallery and show Maybeck's innovative working of Mediterranean themes. He (or the owner) must have delighted in having the creek next to the house, for a redwood sitting bridge (which is private) was placed over the lush creek bed. There's a public bench to the right of the creek, next to an old stone retaining wall and surrounded by young redwoods, palms, and birches. The classically designed building on the corner is a Jesuit rectory.

Farther on Le Roy, come to the small oak in the middle of the street, where Annie Maybeck, Bernard's wife, saved a larger oak from a city destruction crew (see *Berkeley's First Environmental Activist* in the first book), and then an interesting brick and wrought iron building and courtyard, designed by the noted

English architect Ernest Coxhead, opposite #1777. Coxhead was also one of the seminal First Bay Tradition architects.

Round the corner to the right onto Ridge and see another Coxhead original at #2533, with redwood siding joining his characteristic brick and iron. Go to Euclid, past the huge footprints on the sidewalk leading up to a university-related building, turn right, then make another right on Le Conte. The homes, apartment buildings, and offices along here have a settled feeling as you turn left on Le Roy and back to Virginia origins, where the only street names are inscribed on the concrete pavement.

Urban Wildlife

*I*t may sound incongruous, but urban dwellers need wildlife more than any so-called utility. No, its absence would probably not be a threat to human survival, but given the frenetic, jangled nature of the man-made world, it is a powerful and healing thought that wild animals are dispersed throughout the hills, living the simplest, most natural lives imaginable. They eat mostly what they find that day, except for the vegetarians, who do save a few goodies for later. If their homes collapse, they find others. If they are threatened by some external force, they hide until the danger passes, then go on as if nothing ever happened. If they are hot, they find shade. If they are thirsty, they find water. They may not have fun, in a human sense, but I'm sure they don't sit around wondering if they are or not, as humans do. They don't waste time, nor do they check the time, nor do they worry about being on time. They are time, in that their own bodies and brains are also their clocks.

While I get uptight trying to decide between fettucini Alfredo or eggplant Parmesan, wild animals have eaten their suppers and gone to sleep—without any TV, without any phone conversations with friends, without, even, a nighttime snack. And they don't get up two hours later remembering they didn't pay the utility bill.

Some might say, "How can you compare the way wild animals live and how humans live?" And it's true: we have these opposable thumbs, and a cerebral cortex, and an upright spine, and rent to pay every month. But on the other hand, all of us mammals have two eyes, one nose, one mouth, two ears, appendages for locomotion, apparatus for making babies, lungs that breathe the same air, and an appetite. We have feelings and spirit, too, that keep us alive, let us feel fear, sense danger, realize safety, know those who are related to us, care for our offspring, feel pain, feel well-being, enjoy the warmth of the sun, and seek shelter in the rain. These are common to all mammals.

We are, then, brothers and sisters to wild animals. We are attuned and attendant to each other. We have paid, therefore, and do pay now, a great psychic price for killing and harassing them. Our collective wounds are deep, as we grieve on fathomless, unknown levels for the grizzly bear, the kit fox, the cougar, the buffalo, the pronghorn, the condor, the wolf, the coyote, the fox, and the whale. We don't even know how much we grieve, but our spiritually desolate lives reflect the grief. We console ourselves by writing them off as just wild, untamed animals, not worthy of human compassion, care, and concern. We assuage the guilt with rationales that separate us from their world, a world we refer to as so many habitats. Yet their world is our world. Their earth is our earth. Their habitat is our habitat.

It's not my intent for this essay to sound like an intellectual exercise. I feel deep pain over the onslaught against wildlife. My life is the poorer for it. These few words are a meager response to a monstrous injustice. We have run roughshod over nature, and though I do not lead the pack, I am an accomplice of sorts.

Recently while walking the East Bay hills, an owl's hoot greeted me, and I returned the call. The owl answered back, and for a moment, there was kinship. There was understanding and communication. Suddenly the owl swooped down and flew near, as if to acknowledge our inherent camaraderie, remaining since a reminder of kinship of other forms of life on this earth.

We need wildlife . . . and not just on Sierra Club calendars or in coffee-table books. We need them to be there, living simply, with their own brand of dignity on this planet that was created as their — our — hearth, host, and home.

North Berkeley in the 1890s. (PHOTO COURTESY BERKELEY HISTORICAL SOCIETY)

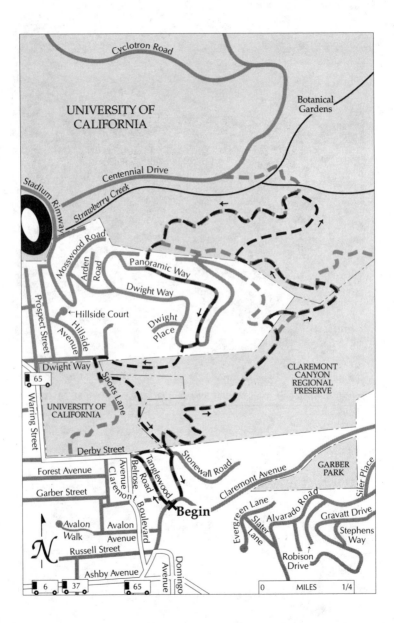

6
Over the Hill &
Through the Woods

Terrain: *steep; rough trails, improved and unimproved paths*
Special Equipment: *hiking shoes, a walking stick if desired, water, snacks*
Bus Lines: *65, 6, 37*
Parks: *John Muir School playground, UC Botanical Gardens, UC sports facility on Dwight Way*
Shops: *Domingo Avenue across from Claremont Hotel, College Avenue*
Distance: *4.5 miles*
Directions: *From I-80, take Ashby Avenue up past Telegraph, past College, to a left on Claremont Boulevard. Stay straight to Tanglewood Road.*

This is not a walk for the out-of-shape, although if taken in small increments, one could get in shape after a few tries. In the first half-mile, the rise in elevation is considerable, and so are the rewards: Panavision Bay Area views, baby cottontail rabbits scurrying off the trail into the brush, dramatic and intriguing trees, birds of prey riding the canyon currents, and a little farther a grove of redwoods that rivals the peace of a deep Sierra forest. There are elegant people-made things as well, like houses at the beginning, middle, and end of this walk.

On Claremont Avenue, opposite the Claremont Hotel and just before the street winds up to the ridges of regional parks, find Tanglewood Road. Claremont Avenue here used to be a quiet wagon road, but it is now a busy shortcut that bypasses the often gridlocked Caldecott Tunnel, gateway to ever-growing Contra Costa County. The picket-fenced colonial at #2820 and the graceful weathered-brick and shingled-roof house next door attest to the street's more sedate and unhurried past. Mature elm trees line the street, like old soldiers.

Tanglewood, too, and its spur street, Garber, have the feel of another time, with great redwoods, mature red horse chestnut trees, with their dark pink spikes of flowers that bloom in spring, classic stucco mansions, and manicured grounds (such as #28, #18, and the Georgian-style house at #10). At the end of Tanglewood, past #3 on the right, climb the concrete steps. The buildings to the left used to be part of the California Schools for the Deaf and Blind and have been tastefully renovated into senior housing by UC Berkeley as part of its Clark Kerr Campus.

The path ascends between a row of cottonwoods and an old weathered fence, opening to a bend at Stonewall Road. Behind are views of the bay, the San Francisco skyline, and the Golden Gate Bridge. To your immediate left is the entrance to Claremont Canyon Regional Preserve, an expanse of greenbelt open space that connects with more wild country owned by UC Berkeley farther up. So tighten your laces, give yourself a little pep talk, and start to climb the trail that threads through the eucalyptus groves up to some of the best views, within walking distance, in the East Bay (we call that a motivator in the walking guidebook profession). One word of caution here: although mountain bikes are officially banned on this steep trail within the preserve, there are some who ignore the rule and come down the hill at very high speeds. Be on the alert for these daredevils and let them know they shouldn't be there.

The trail bends sharply to the right at a small plateau and then begins to rise steeply, veering left and leveling off as views open to the west. A great horned owl has been seen and heard in the eucalyptus trees to the right.

Another eucalyptus grove to the left caps the point that looks out onto all of Berkeley and the open space to the right. Wildfires have raged through here — grass fires in rainless summers. It's a good place to stop for a breather or lunch — this promontory — but on higher is even better if you can wait after the work of the climb to come.

So, if your lunch is all digested, let's get to the climb, which really is great fun. Really! It's a matter of attitude, of perspective, of vision, of perspicacity. Actually, it's a matter of leaning into the hill and keeping the legs moving. Most hearts are designed for this kind of thing, and there's a very good chance you won't die. Drink water along the way, whether you already had your eight glasses or not.

It's not a long way to the top, but foot for foot it may be one of the steepest trails within Berkeley's limits. Listen for a hooting owl, trained as a cheerleader, and imagine the calories burning away with each step.

The trail levels some about a third of the way — a chance to pause and scan the views south of Oakland. The blue among the gray buildings of Oakland is Lake Merritt, the largest saltwater lake within a city in America. At midpoint, a rock to the left gives a good backrest for sitting and surveying your domain, as your loyal subjects struggle to find a place for themselves on jammed freeways and crowded streets.

When all in your relam is deemed in order, begin the final assault of the summit (why are summits always "assaulted"?). Keep in mind that once you've made it to the top, it's almost all downhill for the rest of this walk. And what's coming up is some of the most unusual and inspiring terrain within any city limit anywhere. (And yet another motivator.)

You probably won't notice as you respire to the top, but Scotch broom, mule ears, and poppies line the steep trail, as the gate finally comes into view. (Be particularly aware of outlaw bikers shooting this section of the hill. Listen for the churning sound of rubber on dirt.)

Through the gate, continue on the asphalt road to the right, viewing the oval house to the far left and one of the greatest views of San Francisco Bay behind you. A little farther, another architectural wonder—an amalgam of brick and shingles and birdhouse chimney tops and skylights and craftsman doors—is partially hidden behind hedges to your immediate left. The construction of the house was opposed in the early eighties by some who wanted one of the East Bay's best overviews to be in the public domain.

Bear right, past the house, on the dirt trail to the right of the old machine that looks like it could have started the Industrial Revolution. It's a winch of sorts, or a concrete mixer, or a torture chamber left over from an Inquisition yard sale—if you figure it out, let me know.

Cottontail rabbits often dart off the trail here as you pass a Monterey pine and cypress grove (where you can explore if you like). The trail forks after the grove, but either one will take you to the same place. This dirt road used be part of the Pony Express route to Orinda and was a main route over the hills before the Caldecott Tunnel was built.

Where it begins to rise again sharply, turn left past the "Ecological Study Area" sign (much of this area was planted by UC students and is used for botanical study) and descend steeply, watching your footing as you wind down past digger pines. This leads to a broader dirt trail that is used extensively by joggers and walkers up from the UC stadium complex area—so much so that even though it qualifies in elevation, a "Hi" is rare from anyone here. You might try a one-on-one "Hi" if you'd like to break the "Hi" barrier (see Page 175).

Now bear left, with views of the Lawrence Hall of Science and the UC Botanical Gardens, both fascinating side trips, as the trail snakes downward, with native oak and laurel along the way. After about a quarter mile, the trail widens some, and a dirt path appears on the right. It's next to a pine grove and opposite a peaceful cedar grove on the left. Turn right on the trail, which has been well worn by past travelers, down toward a lush redwood and fern forest.

It's the UC's Woodbridge Metcalf Grove, planted by students in 1926, and providing all the pleasures of the deepest of Sierra forests but a lot closer to home. On a hot day, it's a great place to stay cool. And on a cool, damp day, you can bundle up and smell those primeval smells of wet wood and soil and let the forest embrace you.

Stay on the trail to the right down to the main trail, where a left starts a gentle ascent. A right here will take you to the UC Botanical Garden, and if you have the time it is worth the added couple of miles (see map for details).

It's a gentle climb, with old oaks twisting and turning down the hillside, along with forget-me-nots along the trailside, and occasional cypress and pine trees. The trail ends at Panoramic Way, exiting through the metal posts, high above the campus at this point. Go left under the Bishop pine, and walk the narrow street that feels like a forest trail in places, with bay views to boot.

In a short while, reach the junction with Dwight Way and more wide open views of the bay from south to north. Turn right past the handsome redwood-sided house at #690, and then veer left on an obscure trail that drops into the open space area to the left. It comes in just before the iron guardrail that bends to the right.

Watch your footing — use rocks and clumps of grass to your advantage — as you descend this rough, loose dirt trail, past a red bench with two stumps for legs. A UC playing field and running track is below, as you continue to climb down, always bearing right on the trail and heading toward the track. After a small wind-weathered live oak, the trail follows a ridge leading to wood and dirt steps, which help the hiking. Stay on the trail to the right out to lower Dwight Way, next to the cyclone fence.

Now you have a choice. For those with time, energy, and an interest in architecture, follow the directions in this paragraph. For those with none of the above, skip to the next paragraph and proceed. Continuing on Dwight Way, go right at Hillside Avenue, noting #2444, a brown-shingled house designed and built in 1905, supposedly by Julia Morgan. She also designed #2440 in the same year. Two houses to the right, the Tibetan center, Padma Ling, and #2425 were originally built in 1890, with Morgan adding alterations to the former in 1911. The English architect, Ernest Coxhead, designed #2434 in 1901, and John Galen Howard, founder of UC Berkeley's School of Architecture, did the stucco house at #2428 in 1912, and the classical design at #2422 in 1911. Cross Derby Creek, which you can see from the stone wall on the right, and turn right on Hillside Court, a street that looks the same today as when it was completed more than 70 years ago (it has actually improved with age with its bay laurel, incense cedar, sequoia, coast redwood, Douglas fir, and coast live oak having matured to impressive heights and girths). There is #15 straight ahead, with long imperial shingles, a trellis entryway, and a rosemary-covered retaining wall, designed by John Hudson Thomas in 1907, an example of his early work when he was using wood. And next to it, #19, is the Joseph LeConte House (LeConte was an early mountaineer, succeeding John Muir as president of the Sierra Club), built in 1908, with a symmetrical design by Julia Morgan. To the right, at #14, is another Thomas design, this time with his more characteristic stylized stucco, built in 1914; and yet another Thomas-designed house at #18, built in the same year, with a very small car garage and large barnlike doors, a feature usually relegated to back yards at that time. Coming out of the court, bear left on Prospect Street (to the immediate right you might want to check two very old houses: #2415, built in 1900, and #2405, built in 1883 by Clinton Day, the designer of Falkirk Mansion in San Rafael). Thomas designed #2421, part shingle, part stucco, in 1907, and as you turn left on Dwight Way, Willis Polk, another noted architect of the day, designed two houses for his family at #2903 and #2907. That brings you right back to the location of the next paragraph.

Now go left (right, if you took the preceding minitour) on Sports Lane, then another immediate left on the dirt path with its brick border, rising and joining a concrete walkway to the previously seen track and soccer field. The sign says "No Trespassing," but the college allows the public to use the field, so enter the revolving-door gate, join the other joggers, walkers, and players, and circle the track to the opposite end, where you exit to the right through another gate. Descend past an abandoned concrete stairway to an asphalt and dirt path opposite a drainage basin on the left. Follow this past a eucalyptus grove, through a cyclone gate, and then through another old fence out to the start of Claremont Canyon Regional Preserve, completing the fairly wild loop.

Go down Stonewall Drive to the right, passing sycamore trees and the flower-covered mission-style mansion at #10. The house is worth admiring, with its brick and stucco exterior, red-tile roofs, arches, porches, rose-covered wrought iron gates and rails, and ivy around an array of windows of every shape known. Other houses on this block are noteworthy as well.

Stonewall joins Claremont, where you turn right, passing Tanglewood to the line of elms and New England–like houses. The small gourmet ghetto on Domingo offers rest and refreshment after this long expedition into and through some of Berkeley's most untrammelled walking country.

Coyote

*T*he first time our eyes met, I froze, and so did the coyote. It was on a ridge above Berkeley, midmorning, November, the kind of day that had lured me from the dull, numb Novembers of New Hampshire. I was shocked at first, not at sighting this animal, but that we were so close. The coyote was higher up, on a rocky rise above the trail, and after about 15 seconds, which seemed like an hour, this predator, whose call symbolizes the West, turned and trotted upward and out of sight. My breathing took a heave and continued. So did the memory. I had seen my first coyote in the wild.

A young one, I think — not so wary of human beings. Two hundred years of being tracked, poisoned, and shot, and there was still a soft edge to the eyes, an unhurriedness to the gait. Was the animal injured, or just unafraid? No, there was no injury, I reckoned. It was probably the protectedness of Tilden Park. No guns. No angry ranchers. No pelt hunters. No bounties. A coyote could feel at home.

And this was truly coyote's home. No need for a deed, no building permits, no assessor. There was just a simple life, hunting what was available, taking nothing except to survive. This was not a trickster, not a varmint, not a scurrilous predator, as often branded. This was just coyote, doing what coyotes have done long before humans arrived.

I saw coyote again — I'm sure it was the same animal — at another time near the same spot. It was on the Sea View Trail, the one that loops off the Big Springs Trail and climbs to heaven. It's wide and multiuse (as the recreation technicians refer to it), it is part of the East Bay Skyline National Trail, and its views take in just about everything in four counties.

I saw coyote near the crest — near the circle of stone that some say is an Indian power spot. Power spot or not, it commands a 360-degree view, including Mt. Diablo, Mt. Tamalpais, Sutro

Tower, four bay bridges, and, at certain magical moments, twilight extravaganzas, featuring a setting sun over the Marin hills and a rising moon over Diablo, bathed in an alpenglow sunset sky. There are often lurching tentacles of fog, as well, reaching for Contra Costa but not quite making it down to San Pablo Reservoir.

This was a clear day, windy, clean like ice but warmer. It was morning and coyote gamboled down just in front of the power spot. This time I followed, finally not forgetting my camera when needed most. The wild being stayed enough ahead to remind me this was a wild being. On this day, that wildness involved stalking and hunting some small animal and waltzing through high grass and standing on rocks looking around. I was on my belly, creeping like a lizard, moving only when coyote moved. I knew I'd been noticed, though . . . and tolerated as long as I stayed outside a certain instinctual boundary. It was closer than I'd expected to get, for this was a very trusting wild animal. I was grateful to be permitted entry into this field of dreams.

In this time, our worlds are so coupled. Trust and simplicity must be tempered with wariness and strategy. A road, so convenient and straightforward to me, is a problem to a coyote. It is an obstacle that must be considered in the course of daily events, much different from wild places that don't as often require such an adjustment.

A human analogy would be the collapse of the Cypress structure and the Bay Bridge in the Loma Prieta earthquake. Our migration/commuting patterns were unavoidably altered. We in the East Bay had to take the ferry, or BART, or even the Richmond/San Rafael Bridge to get to the city where the bread was, the prey, the entertainment. And now, to avoid the I-80/580 Berkeley curve megalo-backup, city streets must be taken through neighborhoods hitherto little explored by commuters. South Park Drive in Tilden Park represents the same challenge to coyotes, only *Canis latrans*'s biological clock, so linked to ours, may be ticking faster. It's a matter of territory, and coyote's is rapidly shrinking.

Mountain bikes, too, a source of recreation and fun in my world, are to be avoided in coyote's. Airplanes, electric fences, dogs, and even people talking are commonplace in my world. But in coyote's world, strategic moves must be made. What seemed safe in the morning may now be impassable. A detour may be needed, or a place to lay low for awhile, letting stillness and silence dissolve the intruder with disinterest.

It's easy to forget how this human-created world must appear to wild beings. They have the same kind of nerve endings and gray matter as we, and their senses are even more sensitized from continual use. I respect wild animals because they work at their freedom. They have to. Coyote's freedom has been crimped. Movement is more restricted. Wary eyes scan more, for the unexpected, for the twist within territory which was once, long, long ago, more trustworthy. Coyote has made accommodations and, much more so than man, has been The Great Compromiser.

And what coyote has had to compromise is a part of being wild. Yet it seems not to be a problem. The coyote has adapted well to people. Unlike the cougar, or kit fox, or bear, they have learned to live on the perimeter of our society, and, indeed, although many would not be willing to admit it, coyotes are a part of our society — part of our vernacular landscape.

That coyote is on the run in the Tilden hills is a manifestation of human use on that formerly wild landscape. But like other species under stress from the man-made, coyote is a reminder — a powerful reminder of spirit, free and wild. The coyote is a reminder that survival, and even growth, needn't have certainty for a base. Courage is what's needed, and the wisdom to stay out of harm's way.

I have not seen coyote in Tilden for quite some time now, and to keep my own wildness alive, I need the actual experience of seeing. My social conditioning is too strong only to use visualization. I fear this wild being may have retreated to more remote and distant grounds. There was a murder in Tilden Park last year, and a rape, and a man who was walking naked on a trail near Inspiration Point. I wonder if coyote's nerve endings sensed the increased human violence and insensitivity, and opted for one more adjustment: that of leaving altogether. Even I, a much less sensitive being, have been avoiding this wonderful park as a result of the violence.

I look up at the photograph I took of coyote. There is movement and aliveness in it. In the high grass, rusty, full fur enlightens darker eucalyptus in the background. Coyote plays and pounces, unconcerned. Will our world keep pushing away instead of protecting? Will our world continue to destroy *our* world?

We are so linked, coyote and I. Yet *my* wild nature lies hidden within—hidden beneath a mail of socialization. I roam the hills, hoping to find it. I light my fireplace on hot summer nights. I attend a men's group and beat drums. I eat raw foods. It's not enough. I need coyote . . . to remember. No, I have not seen coyote in the Tilden Hills for a long time, and I feel a little lost.

The Sea View Trail continues beyond the power spot, with its bench and picnic table like thrones above Valhalla, high above the frequent fog line—fog that fills the East Bay bowl like whipped cream—cold whipped cream. Up here, though, it's mostly sun and soaring red-tailed hawks and trusting California newts and plodding darkling "stink" beetles, and speedy Western fence lizards . . . and, after you fork right, off the Sea View back onto the other end of the Big Springs, a couple of great horned owls—if you're lucky . . . and quiet—silhouetted on the evening sky, conversing, while perching in pine trees.

The trail winds back down to the parking lot, encouraging the kind of walking that forces the arms into a free swing. It's hard to resist, and for a moment wildness comes with the swinging and wind in the hair. Somewhere in the hills above or beyond, coyote burrows into a den — to care for pups or eat prey or remember the day and howl both a requiem and refrain in a rhapsody of survival.

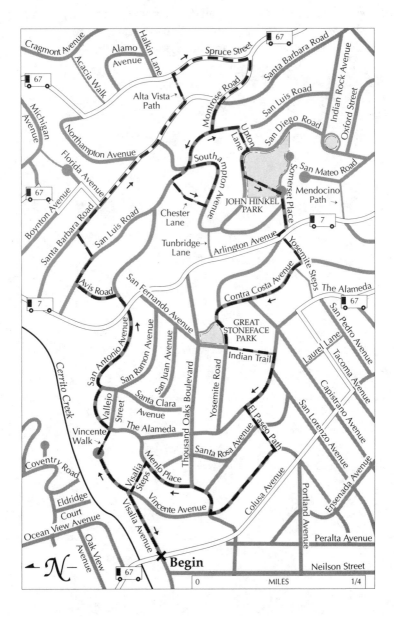

MILES

0   1/4

7

Northern North Berkeley Paths

Terrain: *easy to moderate; developed paths and steps*
Bus Lines: *67, 67A*
Parks: *Veterans Memorial Park, John Hinkel Park, Great Stoneface Park*
Shops: *Solano Avenue, Colusa Avenue in Kensington*
Distance: *3.5 miles*
Directions: *From I-80, take Albany exit, up Solano Avenue to a left at Colusa. Continue to Visalia Avenue, just before the Kensington border.*

P arts of North Berkeley feel so settled that it's easy to forget that its true infrastructure—its oaks, creeks, and the land itself—is in constant change from earthquake activity. The area encompassed in this walk at one time must have seemed insurmountable and remote to those living in the civilized flat lands below. The terrain is hilly, the summer fog thick, and coppices are dark and steep. But today, because of a creative street design that blends nature with the needs of the community, the walker of this far North Berkeley Camelot can experience the best of all possible worlds.

Start on Colusa Avenue, near the Kensington border, at Visalia Avenue, climbing east on Visalia, with live oaks, birches, ornamental fig trees, elegantly simple older stucco houses, and the twin Tudor Revival houses to the left, with their front yards hosting bridges, oaks, buckeye trees, and one of the only visible sections of Cerrito Creek (*cerrito* is Spanish for little hill). The houses were built in the mid-twenties, by an architect who drew inspiration from cottages he saw during a trip to England; and the present owners have the dubious distinction of having to pay taxes to both Alameda and Contra Costa counties, since the backyards are in Kensington, which is part of Contra Costa County.

The creek, which starts in Kensington, can be a wild one, having flooded in the past, but concrete embankments have tamed it in recent years. There is also evidence of an Indian settlement near this spot, since mortars, used to pound oak acorns into meal, were found along the creek here. Heavy metals pollute the winding creek, which eventually flows past the north side of Albany Hill and into the bay. But with the increased interest in urban creeks in the East Bay, perhaps Cerrito Creek will one day be restored to its former purity and prominence.

Continuing around the bend to the left, pass a fabulous passion flower vine, evergreen pittosporum, a handsome Japanese/burlwood fence at #494, along with rock-bound front yards, to a cul-de-sac. Take the steps—the unsigned Vicente Walk—to the right at the end of the street, climbing steeply under oak, fir, spruce, ivy, and Victorian box pittosporum near the top. At The Alameda, a much quieter part of this street than the section near Solano Avenue, veer left, past #534 with its graceful Chinese elms, a semievergreen species, resistant to the deadly Dutch elm disease.

Still ascending, take the sidewalk steps next to a home with an oak seemingly growing out from within it (watch your head!). This leads to the end of The Alameda and the intersection with San Ramon and San Antonio avenues. Stay straight on San Antonio, crossing to the sidewalk for safety. Cerrito Creek flows far below in the brushy canyon to the left. Stucco is the building material of choice along here, influenced by memories of the fire of 1923, which leapt from shingled roof to roof, leveling most of a lower part of North Berkeley. The blue Atlas cedar at #1836 adds to the elegance of this street.

Now use the crosswalk and carefully navigate Arlington Avenue, a once tranquil street that has become a speedway connector between Kensington and Berkeley, to a continuation of San Antonio, with a picturesque English-style cottage on the right, of stone, stucco, and wood, and a weathered, mossy cedar shingle roof.

Bear left at the first street on the left, unsigned Avis Road, where a sweet violin sometimes filters through the Chinese elms lining the street. At San Luis Road, there are persimmon and loquat, and as you turn right, buckeye and pine. A classical pianist often continues the concert, as you go left on an unnamed footpath, just past #597 at a wooden post and street light. It's opposite a stand of tall Monterey pines. Ascend the steps and pathway through a nursery of holly, hydrangea, birch, privet, Japanese maples, and plum trees.

Go right on Santa Barbara Road, past the handsome #647 and tall stands of Monterey pines, past Northampton Avenue and the turrets, steps, and stone chimes of #671, through the mini-pine forest on the left side of the street, past the magnificent grounds and home of #683, past Southampton Avenue, still on Santa Barbara, with views of the city and mountain by the bay. Stay on the sidewalk jungle, which includes podocarpus and the bonsai-looking leptospermum, or Australian tea tree, until you reach Alta Vista Path, just past #731, on the left.

It's an old path, not indicated on local maps, with incense cedar, cracked concrete steps, and wood and iron rails, which you may need for assistance up to higher and busier elevations of Spruce Street. At Spruce, turn right, walking on a sidewalk set back more than usual from the traffic flow, giving the active street a quieter feeling for the walker. At #738, there's a young silver maple and a clinker-brick Tudor with diamond window panes, stained glass, and shuttered windows to further take your attention away from the speeding cars on Spruce. Other attention grabbers include a statue of a woman under a lovely cherry tree at #728, and a gracious Italian stone pine at #720. The evergreen grand magnolia, the deciduous southern magnolia, hawthorne, and more cherry trees add to the landscape.

Turn right on Montrose Road, with its camphor street trees, to a winding descent, with Mt. Tamalpais views, and, after crossing Santa Barbara, a storybook cottage on the corner with turrets and spires, an oblique shingled roof, and a rooster weathervane. Continuing on Montrose, look to the left to telescopic views of the Golden Gate Bridge and the San Francisco skyline. Bear right on San Luis Road, passing Hampton, then Southampton, under several California buckeye trees.

Now look for Chester Lane, with sign, just past the ivy-covered, brick Tudor at #690, and descend to the left under the delicate yellow-flowered azara, live oak, cedar, birch, Monterey pine, and large redwoods near the bottom, on the grounds of a classic stucco Tudor Revival estate on the left. Take a moment to admire the whole pleasing interplay of house and landscape.

Then go left on Southampton, with more camphor trees (providing great shade but cracking the sidewalk with their invasive roots), getting a closer look at the abovementioned house at #131, as well as most of the other houses realtors would today call "Old World Charm." One of them, though, the Joralemon House at #168, deserves closer attention: the stucco house was designed by Bernard Maybeck just after the 1923 fire, and uses semifireproof materials, including copper flashing. The fire actually revived Maybeck's career, since he was 60 at the time and preparing to wind down his activities. He was so much in demand, though, that this began an entirely new facet of his work. This house, with its Mediterranean stucco styling, arched windows, and inviting entrance way, is a good example of his thinking at the start of the final phase of this creative genius's life.

Turn right on San Luis, passing Montrose, and a line of old Dutch elm–diseased elms, then make a right on Upton Lane, with a sign, just before #768. It's a steep, intriguing descent on concrete steps—no railing—naturally accompanied by blackberry vines, fan palms, and a thick stand of bamboo, exiting onto San Diego Road, with a nicely designed rose garden to the left.

Cross San Diego and go right, skirting John Hinkel Park on the left and a row of Lombardy poplar to the right. At the old lamppost, enter the park to the left, with its clubhouse, built in 1911 and still in use, to the left. Weave downward (or explore other sections, including Blackberry Creek and paths following the contours of the terrain) under oak, laurel, and pittosporum, through the picnic and playground area to the right, to an asphalt path and concrete steps leading down to the quiet intersection of Southampton and Somerset Place, graced by the tucked-away English-style cottage at #2, with its steep-sloping shingle roof. The house was built in 1925.

Follow Somerset out to Arlington Avenue, go right and cross via the stone steps, just past the pedestrian crossing sign, to the median strip, then carefully cross the Arlington speedway again. You're now at the junction with Yosemite and its small park on the corner, with benches and tiny lawn.

Cross Yosemite to the west side and find the Yosemite Steps—a signpost but no sign—just past #1992, and descend to the left, under an old late-bearing apple tree, to always-inspiring bay and San Francisco views. At the first street you come to (the steps continue down to The Alameda from here but are not included on this particular walk), which is sleepy Contra Costa Avenue, go right, passing Capistrano, up to Yosemite Road, where you veer left. (You may wish to take a short architectural diversion here and go right on Yosemite to visit four houses designed by John Hudson Thomas in 1928, at #1941 through #1947, and a Julia Morgan creation at #1962, built in 1920.)

Yosemite bends to the left, past #1924, designed in 1916 by its architect/owner Noble Newsome, another noted designer of that era, past volcanic rock gardens of blue spruce, rhododendron, and azalea, then the Great Stoneface Park on the right, a site Ohlone Indians used for centuries as an encampment (*Ohlone* means western people and is the name most preferred by present-day descendants). They may have also used (or blazed) the Indian Trail, marked by a sign opposite the San Fernando/Yosemite sign. (This path is in the first book as well, and it is one of my favorites.)

The path should be walked slowly and quietly, savoring old-brick construction, stepping stones, and even a small cave about half way down, looking back to the right (which I missed in prior research). At the bottom is The Alameda and an old huge decorative urn. Go right, past the stately grounds and brick and wood house at #715, a Henry Gutterson design, built in 1915 (he was an associate of Maybeck's at one time), past San Lorenzo, past #671, built in 1912 and questionably attributed to John Hudson Thomas, to the El Paseo Path, to the left, next to #650. Walk down to San Miguel Avenue, cross and continue on stone steps, under a dark, verdant canopy, to Vincente Avenue.

Turn right on Vincente, with olive trees, and the wisteria-laced Craftsman bungalow at #636, displaying the versatility of John Hudson Thomas, who definitely did design this one in 1913. Enjoy, too, bay views to the left, and a huge volcanic boulder and Zen-spirited garden, with its bonsai black pine, to the right. Bear right on Thousand Oaks Boulevard, crossing the street and continuing up, past San Miguel, with the elegant Grecian-style house on the corner. Go left at Menlo Place, with more Grecian styles, turrets, red-tile roofs, and balconies, passing Santa Rosa Avenue and its coast live oak gracing the street, an example of a more sensitive time when trees were figured into the landscape architect's street design. The house at #69 was designed by Julia Morgan in 1915. (By the way, she also designed the handsome Thousand Oaks Baptist Church at Colusa and Catalina near Solano.)

Just past #59, go left on the Visalia Walk, down its steps flanked by oak, ivy, volcanic rock, and a split-rail fence, to Vincente Avenue. Cross and stay straight on Visalia Avenue to Mt. Tam views, and the creekside houses at #1651 and #1641 noted at the beginning. The three-and-a-half-mile hike ends where it began, at Colusa, with liquidamber (colorful in the fall and early winter), camphor trees (which actually smell of camphor if you sniff a recently cut branch), and Cerrito Creek (to which you can bid adieu from a stone wall, to the right, on Colusa just short of the Kensington border, as it flows on to the bay).

Birds

*I*f you're ever walking on Telegraph in Berkeley, or Piedmont in Oakland, or Throckmorton in Mill Valley, stop for a moment and listen. Up above the noise of the street, in the trees, a chorus often gathers, singing at full volume — a chorus of songbirds — reminders that where all our streets and buildings and wires and poles are, wilderness once was. Mankind can cut down trees to let more light into living rooms, can bury parks under parking lots, and dam, divert, and force streams underground, but there's less that can be done about birds. Despite our assault on wildness, birds continue to live among us (although, according to the scientists, alarmingly reduced in number).

That they've survived the past 200 years is extraordinary. Where most other wild species have left or have become extinct in the wake of noise, exhaust fumes, industrial and domestic wastes, and commercial construction and housing, birds have stayed close, persevering, adapting to our abuses. And not only do they stay, but they sing and soar quite joyfully, it seems.

If you stop for a moment, and quiet the internal chatter, you can hear sounds that were here long before human technology came, and will be here long after technology crumbles. Bird song can penetrate the noise of both motor and mind, but only if there is a hearer willing to harvest the sounds of this moment.

There are two birds that have a particular impact for this walker. They are quiet birds, so the impact is more visual than auditory. One is the hummingbird, who seems to have such fun with life. Even its work of food gathering looks like play, like the neon-green Anna's hummingbird at a cool waterfall one day. As it perched on a protruding rock, it repeatedly stuck its needle beak into the water, seemingly titillated by the movement of the water, as it leapt off the rock often to dip and sip, flying away then returning, absorbed in the play of it. Its work and play were the same, fully integrated. How would that be to live with such lightness and joy?

The other is the red-tailed hawk, gliding and soaring high above the houses and streets, up in the hills. The red-tailed must be at play, too—a wind bird, so skilled in flight that it wastes not an erg. How would it be to fly with the hawk? To be without the burden of effort, of struggle, allowing the currents of life to set the course? The red-tailed responds to the changes of wind, almost instantaneously, not out of habit or knowledge, but from its oneness with the wind. It responds to the wind and chooses which way to fly—swiftly, effortlessly, simply.

Is it possible to live as the hummingbird and hawk do? To come right up to the face of life and sip its water, or soar with changing currents? To see with a fresh eye, hear with an innocent ear, think with a unfettered mind?

As the hummingbird, hawk, and songbird show, life can be fun—even the daily routines. It's a matter of singing, sipping, soaring, without a moment's doubt, with total trust in the truth of the present.

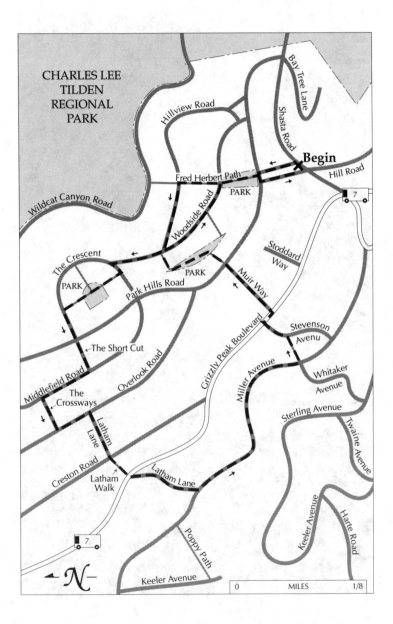

CHARLES LEE
TILDEN
REGIONAL
PARK

Hillview Road

Bay Tree Lane

Shasta Road

Begin

Hill Road

Fred Herbert Path

PARK

7

Wildcat Canyon Road

Woodside Road

Stoddard
Way

The Crescent

PARK

Park Hills Road

PARK

Muir Way

The Short Cut

Overlook Road

Grizzly Peak Boulevard

Stevenson
Avenu

Miller Avenue

Whitaker
Avenue

Middlefield Road

The
Crossways

Sterling Avenue

Twaine Avenue

Latham
Lane

Creston Road

Latham
Walk

Latham Lane

Keeler Avenue

Harte Road

Poppy Path

7

N

Keeler Avenue

0   MILES   1/8

8
Park Hills & Lanes

Terrain: *easy; maintained and unmaintained paths and stairways*
Bus Line: *#7*
Parks: *Tilden Regional, including Environmental Nature Center, the Little Farm, and Botanical Gardens*
Shops: *Walnut Square at Shattuck and Vine*
Distance: *2+ miles*
Directions: *From I-80, take Albany exit, going east on Marin, past The Alameda, to Marin Circle. Bear right on Los Angeles Avenue, then left on Spruce. At Grizzly Peak Boulevard, go right, past Marin, to Shasta Gate.*

As Berkeley grew, houses and streets went higher and higher into the hills. In fact, if the regional parks hadn't been set aside in the thirties, the area encompassing Tilden Park today might have been just one more place to shop. This walk is near one of the highest points of elevation in the East Bay hills: the 1,759-foot monolith (OK, so it's not a monolith, but compared to sea level it's pretty high) Grizzly Peak, located in Tilden Park, near its South Gate, and just above the Grizzly Peak Trail, a couple of miles from where this walk starts.

And where it does start is at the Shasta Gate of Tilden Park, just off Grizzly Peak Boulevard, and across from the formal entrance to the Park Hills housing subdivision, developed by Mason McDuffie Realtors in the early fifties. It is a nicely designed neighborhood, with more style, character, and walking lanes than most post–World War II housing projects.

Heading through the entrance columns at Shasta Gate and Park Gate, pass the row of flowering crab apple trees on either side, cross Park Hills Road at the crosswalk, with views of the Tilden hills, and walk down the Fred Herbert Path straight ahead. The railroad-tie steps and wooden rails were made to last, as was the path's sign, and pines and redwoods provide shade and natural elegance as you reach a small hidden playground with a slide and swings, and a border of wild grasses, flowers, and ivy.

Cross Woodside Road farther down, then continue on the Herbert Path, past hidden houses, under a spreading conifer, and all the time being serenaded by bird song. At the very quiet Hillview Road, go left (the Herbert Path continues down to Wildcat Canyon Road, but that busy street, which has no sidewalk, is generally unsafe for walkers). This leads to Woodside Road as you pass pines, cedar, toyon, shake-shingle roofs, and redwood gates.

At Woodside, climb the railroad-tie steps to the left, opposite the street junction, then walk right, past the colonial-style home at #1088 and more Tilden views, coming to The Crescent Road in a short distance. Turn left here and, just beyond #56, veer right onto an unmarked asphalt path between two hedges, directly opposite the large fir tree across the street. There are fences on either side, as the path opens to another hidden playground, with lawn, benches, basketball court, a redwood jungle gym, and other equipment to keep children busy for awhile. It's a place you could spend a whole day at with a good book or writing project and the time to enjoy it.

When ready, continue straight on the same path to steps leading down to the other side of The Crescent. Turn left, crossing Park Hills Drive to The Short Cut, which sounds like it should be a footpath but is actually a small connecting street.

At Middlefield Road, graced with maple, pine, jasmine, cedar, and birch, go right, then a left at The Crossways, which is also a path-sounding but fully paved street.

At Overlook Road, use caution as you turn left. It's a sharp corner, with no sidewalk, and cars often turn here, so up your awareness meter a notch. A right on Latham Lane, past more appealing street trees, brings you to Creston Road. Here, straight ahead, find the camouflaged Latham Walk, a dirt path to the left of the brick garden fence of #1048 and next to utility pole #832B. It's fairly obscure but, once found, will lead you down to Grizzly Peak Boulevard on railroad-tie steps.

At Grizzly Peak, cross this speedway street very carefully and quickly (no crosswalk here) to Latham Lane, across to the left, and descend past older homes, a eucalyptus grove, and privet hedge trimmed to accommodate short walkers. Bear left on Miller Avenue, glimpsing bay views between the houses and hedges and picking up the sporadic sidewalk on the west side of the street. Round the bend, passing nondescript houses, and go right on a dirt path, just past #1129, at the white fire hydrant. It's opposite Whitaker Avenue and rises up to Stevenson Avenue.

A left takes you up past an older Craftsman redwood house of the First Bay Tradition, with its crazy-quilt shingle roof. This is actually #1130 Grizzly Peak Boulevard. To the right, cross at Muir Way, continuing straight, with expansive views of Tilden Park. Cross Park Hills Road straight ahead to the stairway to the right of #1077. Hedges line the way as the shady lane drops to yet another very hidden public park—a large grassy area with views of the hills and lots of quiet.

To exit the small park, find a couple of manhole covers to the far left and an asphalt and wood path just past the small weathered wood-slat fence. This public path cuts between two houses and leads out to Woodside Road, where a right leads back to the Fred Herbert Path, just past the house and Japanese-style garden of #1130. The steps zigzag back up to the tiny playground, where the delicate English daisy, which opens in the daytime, and closes at night, proliferates. You could make quite a nature study with forget-me-nots, poppies, plantain, and tall grasses rounding out the mini-botanical garden. Avoid the hedges near the steps though, as poison oak is present.

Ascend the remaining steps and stones to Park Hills Road and the Park Gate entrance to Park Hills, a well-planned neighborhood that has aged and ripened since 1952.

First Rain

For the last two years, the first rain fell like down feathers. It would have been nice to walk nude in it, but alas, the Bay Area, and this walker, have grown more conservative over the years. So a rain parka had to do—the very need for protection, a dubious need indeed.

It was barely more than a fog, this rain. And yet a fog was the stuff of summer. No, this was not a fog. A fog moves, roils unsettled in swirls, rushing towards the hills. A fog is asymmetrical. You never know where it will turn next. You can escape a fog in the East Bay—in Tilden Park, high in the hills on the Sea View Trail. From that aerie, it's a hidden Berkeley, filled up with fog to the ridgetops.

But this rain—this first rain—was more than a fog. It was still. It was settled. It was secure in its mission: to deliver the message of winter's salvation. The message of rain: a reminder that the land of California is what it is today because of rain and snow. Take away rain and California would be a desert. People know this, and worry, as we go into our fourth year of drought.

The weatherpeople and water managers will tell us it is not enough, this rain. They will tell us we are so many inches below normal, as they shake their doomsayer heads. Yet this first rain is a hopeful event. Despite all the rain we'll need to make up for the drought, this first rain is a herald, and its message is no more complicated, and no less awesome, than the familiar simple sentence we all use so glibly: "It's raining."

They will close South Park Drive in Tilden Park today, for when it rains, California newts start to migrate across the road to their mating and spawning pools. This rain, then, is very important to newts, helping fulfill something ancient and alive. Their species will continue, which, on some level, newts must know, feeling the benediction of this rain with every pore and nerve.

The rain as benediction. It doesn't signal that we head to our mating grounds, but as it does to the newt, it moistens and settles on our skin, after months of unsettling dry. It is a reminder of a watery composition, a time when we all breathed like fish in our mother's amniotic fluid. So is there really a need to protect against it?

The drought has heightened awareness of it, like absence does of a good old friend. This first rain seems to caress the earth, and its rivulets run like tears — tears of deep communion with living things that marvel at it rather than measure it.

Oakland

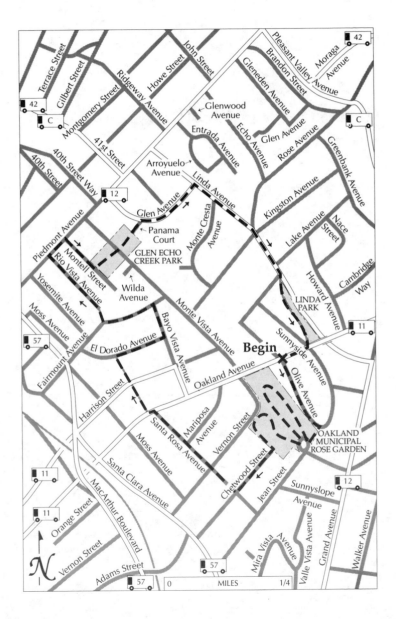

9

Through the Rose Garden & up Glen Echo Creek

Terrain: *easy to moderate; developed paths and stairways*
Bus Line: *11*
Parks: *Beach School, Oakland Rose Garden, Lake Merritt, Piedmont Park, Mountain View Cemetery*
Shops: *Piedmont Avenue, Grand and Lakeshore avenues*
Distance: *3.5 miles*
Directions: *From 580 East, take Oakland Avenue/Harrison Street exit, go left on Oakland Avenue up to Olive Avenue. From 580 West, take Harrison/MacArthur exit, turn right on Oakland to Olive.*

The Great Depression was certainly a dark time in our history, but things were made less bleak by the building of a number of quiet, relaxing parks in the midst of market crashes and bank closings. The Oakland Municipal Rose Garden, built in 1934 by the federal Works Projects Administration (WPA), was such a park, and it continues to provide a haven, where you can promenade down an avenue of roses, close to, but far removed in spirit from, a busy, worrisome, complex world.

This walk starts on Olive Avenue at Oakland Avenue, the major thoroughfare that connects Oakland with Piedmont, just before

Grand Avenue. On the right side of Oakland Avenue, walk along Olive Avenue, either on the sidewalk on the left or the dirt walkway on the right, passing the conical, clinker-brick chimney at #160, to the inlaid concrete steps to the right, next to #300, where Olive veers left.

Walk down under an evergreen canopy to Jean Street and turn right to the porticoes of the Oakland Municipal Rose Garden. A poem by John Masefield, a former poet laureate of England, is inscribed in the commemorative plaque at the entrance:

Roses are beauty but I never see
Those blood drops from the burning heart of June
Glowing like thought upon the living tree
Without a pity that they die so soon.

Now turn up your sensory meter as you walk past roses such as Sierra Glow, Mon Cheri, and Touch of Class, and tea roses such as Tiffany and Sheer Bliss. Pass the reflecting pool, the mission-style rest rooms, and the Mother of the Year Walk, with commemorative stones embedded in the center of the walk for each winning mother since 1954, and spaces-in-waiting for all-star mothers to come. I looked, but could find no corresponding walk for fathers. (In a sociological note, after the standard "Mrs.," all the mothers since 1979 referred to themselves by their own first names, whereas before that most used their husband's first names.)

Continue around the key and then back along the path, this time to the right of the pool, admiring the sometimes cascade to the right that flows down from the wedding site (we'll be back here in a little while). Walk back to the entrance, but this time, enter the portico to the left, go up the steps, jagging left and climbing to the asphalt path straight ahead. This is another, less visited part of the Rose Garden, traversing through a forest of redwood, oak, and pine. At a clearing, young cypress and juniper take over, as you pass steps to the right, rounding the bend, past more cypress, leading to the wedding site.

Now circle the site (if there's a wedding going on, skip to the next paragraph and proceed), with its benches, views, towering Italian stone pines, and more roses. Around the circle, take the few steps leading to the center of the site and continue down one of the pathways on either side of the center cascade, imagining, perhaps, yourself part of a wedding procession as you promenade.

At the bottom, turn left, and ascend the gradual steps with center rail to Vernon Street. But rather than exit here, bear left, past the gate, on the asphalt path leading up and above the wedding site, giving you an even better overview. Stay right, under plum and redwood trees along with views of East Bay hills, on the path which runs beside the apartment house out to Chetwood Street. Go right on this older street, perhaps tasting some blackberries if the season is right, and visually tasting the distinctive Victorian at #648, and the brown-shingled First Bay Tradition house at #644, with its palm and redwood nicely placed in the front yard.

At Santa Clara Avenue, walk right, in this neighborhood first developed about 80 years ago. Notice particularly the modern barn motif at #223 and the shingled #202 as you cross Vernon Street. Now duck under toyon, with its bright red berries, as it forms a trellis over the sidewalk. Across the street is a large deodar cedar tree partially hiding a just as old brown-shingled house.

Cross Mariposa Avenue, passing a row of birch, and coming to busy Oakland Avenue, with Victorian and Georgian mansions across the street. Go left, crossing Santa Clara, then on the other side of Oakland Avenue (no crosswalk here, but it's a one way street, making it fairly easy to navigate) find a footpath to the left of the modern apartment building at #601. There's more toyon (a.k.a. Christmasberry) on this path—along with brown-shingled houses and plum and redwood trees—which emerges on Harrison, another easy-to-cross one-way street. The pathway continues to the right of the lattice fence, and left of #3801, passing hawthorne and, farther down, pine trees, which have paved the path with a soft carpet of needles.

The lane ends at the next street, El Dorado Avenue, where a right takes you past acacia and liquidamber (the tree developed specifically to give northern California fall colors). At Bayo Vista Avenue, turn left on this woodsy street to another left onto Fairmount Avenue. Walking on the right side, go right on a footpath opposite the sign for Rio Vista Avenue and beside an iron fence along the sidewalk.

The verdant path leads to the continuation of Rio Vista, where you'll find simple Victorians and a magnificent stone pine in front of #56. At Piedmont Avenue, which in some ways still retains the flavor of an old-time neighborhood shopping district, turn right, past a noteworthy Southwestern art shop, which has the quality of a museum.

Go right on the next street, Montell Street, passing a row of nicely designed, albeit homogenous, modern brown-shingled houses, a huge, very odorous rosemary plant at #50, and yucca trees at #62. Opposite #65, find the Glen Echo Creek Park to the left and enter the path along free-flowing Glen Echo Creek, bordered by redwood, oak, and a ginkgo tree near the next street (the ginkgo is a living fossil among trees, dating back about 165 million years).

Now cross Monte Vista Avenue, where the park and path continue up to Panama Court, a quiet cul-de-sac leading to Glen Avenue. (There is a neighborhood group, by the way, that has formed to preserve Glen Echo Creek Park, which has been threatened by development over the years. They are also attempting to replace all non-California native trees in the park with native varieties.)

At Glen, bear right, past the mulberry tree on the corner, admiring older, stylish apartment houses at #67 and #66. Go right at the end of Glen onto Linda Avenue, where a large redwood has survived, and stay on this fairly busy street for a bit, crossing the large intersection at Kingston Avenue, then Lake Avenue. Sycamore is the predominant street tree along here.

Just beyond Lake, take the asphalt path to the right into small Linda Park, a shady spot, bordered by Italian stone pine, oak, holly, acacia, western hemlock, a stone bench, views of the Piedmont hills, and the mission-style Beach School and its recreational facilities (including a well-equipped public playground) below. This exits at Oakland Avenue, where a right takes you across Sunnyside Avenue, alongside sycamore and elm trees, back to Olive Avenue and the Oakland Rose Garden. As at the start, it's a good place to rest, sit in the sun, smell a few more roses, and think of whom you might nominate for the next mother of the year, before heading home.

Flowers

O f all the living things you will encounter on a walk, flowers will perhaps touch you deepest. They are the universe dancing. But to really see their dance, you need to dance with them.

Without attention to the dance, they are just pretty flowers, casually noted in passing, as a bright teapot would be noticed in the hardware store window. If we're incessantly talking or thinking or "exercising," we miss the dance. We miss the smell of jasmine, the grace of the columbine, the innocence of the daisy. We may carry our nature guides and studiously learn the names, but we still miss the flowers dancing.

Flowers are expansive. They don't hold back what they're here to give. They don't *decide* to give out their beauty. They give it, and they give it freely, without the slightest hesitation. And in living so, flowers are the epitome of joy.

Walking among flowers, there is an awareness that to really commune with them, there has to be a certain purity that comes with an absence of desire. There is just being present, neither wanting nor rejecting, but experiencing. Flowers are sensitive, scientists tell us, perhaps even to a grasping nature. Could they know when they are being coveted, and sense the moment before they are plucked? Could beings of such beauty, simplicity and delicateness be affected even by thought?

Flowers are innocent, and to be innocent is to be without contention, which is why flowers don't get much press. They have no schemes or plans or axes to grind. They don't wait for city council meetings before deciding, or getting a permit, to grow. They don't subdivide.

Fortunately, many Bay Area residents plant flowers—and nature itself seeds and reseeds its wild offspring. While most of the country's gardens go dormant under winter cold and

snow, here, flowers grow year round—which, for this walker,
means more opportunities to join the dancing.

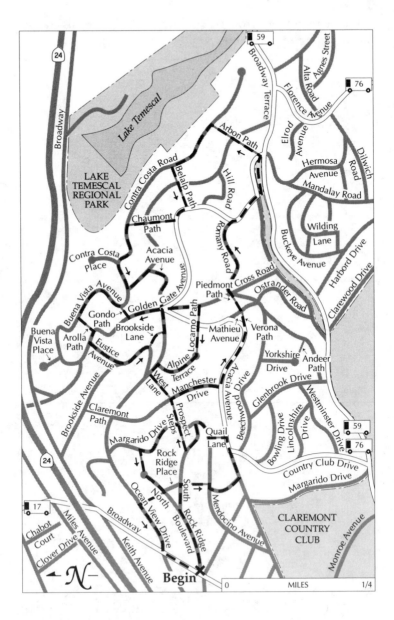

10

Rock Ridge Ridges

Terrain: *moderate to steep; improved lanes and steps*
Bus Line: *17*
Parks: *Lake Temescal, Mountain View Cemetery*
Shops: *College Avenue, Piedmont Avenue*
Distance: *5 miles*
Directions: *From 580 East, take Route 24 toward Walnut Creek. Exit at Broadway, before the tunnel, and turn right to Rock Ridge Boulevard, a few blocks down on the left.*

Like North Berkeley, the streets of Rock Ridge conform to the contours of the hillside. And like North Berkeley, those streets are often connected by lanes and steps, originally to make the foot traveling easier and aesthetically pleasing. But unlike North Berkeley, the homes are not the epitome of the simple home expounded by Keeler and crafted by Maybeck, Morgan, and Gutterson. This area, developed in 1909, was the first East Bay subdivision after the 1906 earthquake and fire. The developers called it Rock Ridge Estates and, as in the nearby Claremont subdivision, targeted wealthy San Franciscans who might consider relocating to the "safer" East Bay.

The first house on the block, at #6025, was a brown-shingle, with exposed structural beams and broad eaves, in the First Bay Tradition. But subsequent house designers veered away from this rustic style, following instead more classical lines — more removed from nature than North Berkeley hillside architecture, but perhaps appropriate for urban Oakland. On one major score, though, Rock Ridge developers and residents were similar to their North Berkeley counterparts: they were pro-pedestrian, designing a neighborhood with walkers and lovers of hidden walkways in mind. This is a long, rather strenuous walk that could be creatively shortened after studying the map and reading the description. If you walk for exercise, and can handle a higher heart beat, this could become one of your favorite routes.

At the upper end of Broadway at Rock Ridge Boulevard, start by walking through the monolithic white Grecian-style entrance monuments, draped with palms, and a deodar cedar to the left. On one occasion, a local family was scraping ivy off the pillars and preparing to enliven them with fresh paint, all on their own time and expense. They explained that the monuments are on private property, absolving the city from maintenance responsibilities. The sidewalks through the monuments are actually easements, allowing public access. The residents in the immediate area share the maintenance cooperatively.

The street was originally planted with palms, and there are still some remaining, with cedar, juniper, pyracantha, and liquidamber used for replacements. Continuing, bear right at Rock Ridge Boulevard South, taking the path and steps to the right opposite Rock Ridge Place and to the left of #6095. The small, triangular park in the middle of this junction hosts palms, spruce, cedar, and a couple of mature California sycamores (which aren't seen very often).

Climb past fig, pear, juniper, cedar, acacia, privet, and papaya to Margarido Drive. Turn right, then cross and bear left on Margarido with bay, Marin headland and hill views, antique lampposts, pine, and redwoods. Bend left at Acacia Avenue, and lean into this quiet street with no sidewalk.

Surrounded by Italianate and Spanish-style houses, pass Country Club Drive and #5900, a mission-style, artfully landscaped with black pine, deodar cedar, lemon, and a border garden. Go left on Quail Lane, a signed pathway and steps to the right of #5922. Descend to both East Bay hill and bay views (one of the few spots that takes in both), along with enough golden bamboo to warrant bringing your pet panda next time.

At the bottom is Margarido, where a right takes you past cedar, oak, Monterey pine, and willow. After a short way, cross and make a hairpin left on Rock Ridge Boulevard South. This snakes down past Tudor and Mission Revivals, grand magnolias, palms, pine, and redwoods to the Prospect Steps, with sign, just past #6150. Go right, following the driveway/right-of-way, then steeply up the steps under Washington thorn and palms to Margarido. Cross and continue up more steps, bordered by bottle brush, hydrangea, fuchsia, blackberries (which are tasty when ripe in the summer), plum, privet, and papaya.

At Manchester Drive, you're greeted by a stately brick Georgian estate. Turn right, as the grade levels, walking past bottlebrush street trees and a winsome cluster of three cut-leaf, or Swedish birches (*Betula pendula 'Dalecarlica'*). Bear left onto Acacia Avenue, with more birch, cooing mourning doves, and, although on private property, a huge ancient chunk of volcanic ash behind the fence and grounds signed "Cactus Rock" to the left. It's another reminder to give thanks for public lands set aside for all to enjoy.

Rounding the bend, see the Verona Path, across the street to the right, directly next to the English Tudor house at #620. This drops down to tiny Mathieu Avenue, where the steps continue as the Piedmont Path, to the right across the street. At the bottom are mature cedar and pine trees and Romany Road, where a left brings you to the intersection with Cross Road and a continuation of Romany to the right.

Follow Romany as it winds on a level grade past oak, spruce, and redwood, and hillside views to the east, eventually merging into Golden Gate Avenue. Bear right, as this soon joins busy

Broadway Terrace and a small median strip/park of cedar and redwood separating you from most of the traffic. Continuing to the left, find the Arbon Path, just past #6190, and begin a long ascent back into the heart of Rock Ridge, as traffic noise subsides. Plants and drought-parched backyards take precedence as the steps thread higher, past Buena Vista Avenue, past a California fan palm (*Washingtonia*), past grand magnolia, acacia, oak, and blackberry, and finally up and out to Contra Costa Road.

Go left on Contra Costa to the Belalp Path, just past #6101, and opposite the house with the rustic cedar shake-shingle roof. A left on the Belalp Path leads you down shady steps to Buena Vista, where you cross and continue through an urban forest of redwood, poplar, oak, and pine to Golden Gate Avenue. Bear right, along this fairly busy street to the Chaumont Path, which you'll find, without a sign, next to #5224. It starts to the right just past the mailbox as steps and a rose-colored path. (Since this is another long, gradual ascent, some of you may wish to skip this part of the walk and continue on Golden Gate to where you'll end up in a short while anyway. The only major thing you'll be missing is the exercise up this long hidden stairway and some views coming down.)

The Chaumont Path climbs a bit more gradually than the previous Arbon, past colorful trumpet vines, morning glories, and bougainvillaea. Cross Buena Vista, staying on the steps with the surreal-looking passion flower on the fence, and Japanese maples, lilies, and nasturtiums completing the landscape. At the top is Contra Costa Road again, where, just past a young sycamore tree, magnanimous views open to the west.

At Contra Costa Place, veer left, past cedar and pepper trees, then left on Buena Vista, with its row of mature yellow poplars, or tulip trees, growing successfully. At Acacia Avenue, cross and bear right, walking down past birch and old deodar cedars.

Around the bend, feast your eyes on the dazzling irregular shingle roof of the corner house.

Approaching the five-corner intersection, stay on Golden Gate and soon find the short Gondo Path to the right, next to #5500. The steps with the iron center rail take you to Buena Vista and its *buena vistas* of the hills. The street winds along an ivy-bordered sidewalk, past the most common of the Pacific Coast's maples, and the only one harvested commercially, the bigleaf, or Oregon, maple. There's also a modern redwood house at #5816 that must have been Maybeck-influenced, with its balconies and long, deep eaves.

As the street bends left, notice London planes and a mature deodar cedar, and then the Arolla Path to the left next to #5757. Descend past redwoods and, at this writing, a barking, though safely fenced, dog. You're now back to Golden Gate at the bottom, where a right leads to Eustic Avenue to the left.

It's a woodsy street, with a eucalyptus grove to the right and left, along with oak and fig, among others. At Brookside Avenue, bear left, past the old English Tudor revival at #6376, to the concrete pillars and steps next to #6394. Local maps call this the Brookside Lane, although, as of this writing, it has no sign at this end.

The forest thickens as you rise—acacia, plum, pine, redwood, cedar, and nasturtium, complete with resident humingbirds. At the landing, once resplendent stone benches now lie broken and covered with graffiti like some B-movie about the fall of Rome. Nonetheless, the benches are usable and would make a good picnic spot on a hot day.

At the top is Ocean View Drive. Go left, then cross Acacia and veer right onto Cross Road at the five corners. An old eucalyptus guards the entrance to the intersection. Dropping sharply, find the Locarno Path, with a sign, just past #255. It's another Grecian-style walkway that is slowly falling to the Visigoths of time, lack of care, and earthquakes. At Acacia, cross and complete the now-shady Locarno Path out to Alpine Terrace, a sunny cul-de-sac with ordered gardens and meticulous houses styled colonial, Italianate, mission, and modern. Views take in two major cities and the bridge that connects them.

At Ocean View turn left and, in a short distance, left again, onto West Lane, next to #6147 and opposite Brookside Avenue. Coming up and over the crest, you understand why this was named West Lane, as most of the Bay Area west opens into view. Duck under the cedar and descend to even wider bay views, down to steps and Manchester Drive. Cross and continue down the steep steps to the right of #5975 to Margarido.

Across Margarido, go right on the recessed sidewalk, somewhat hidden and below street level, past gardens of ice plants (an introduced species, by the way, not native California as many assume), marguerites, juniper, and cedar, next to neoclassic houses to a path and steps just past #6033. Turn left and descend. (As of this writing, there is a somewhat threatening dog who roams the territory at the top of these steps. However, he's a bit of a Johnny-come-lately who doesn't seem to hear you until you're well on your way down, and then won't follow past the top step. Maybe advancing years warn him he'll have to climb back up.)

At the bottom is the cul-de-sac Rock Ridge Boulevard North and its Phoenix palms, one of which is completely covered in a parka of English ivy. Just past this tree, go right on a path next to #6100, past olive, palm, pittosporum, ivy, and another barking, although this time fenced, dog. This path climbs to Ocean View Drive, which probably had more ocean views in 1909, but still affords a glimpse beyond the Golden Gate.

A left on Ocean View leads down to Broadway, where another left, with a background of city skylines, brings you back to the white monument start of this minimarathon.

Walking Together

O ccasionally, I walk these neighborhood footpaths with a close friend or give an out-of-town relative a taste of the Bay Area behind the Bay Area. And there is an entirely different quality in walking together compared with walking alone. Many details around, above, and below get lost in the social contacting. But that social contact becomes richer in the context of that detailed background. Specific flowers may go unseen, but human beings walking together, relating, laughing, sharing can add to the environment—really are part of the environment.

It's not so easy though. We all have different paces, a different inner sense of time, different desire systems and needs. Walking together is like an orchestra of separate musicians, and how skillful the symphony depends on how much each member is able to maintain individual talents, while sacrificing individuality for the common good. And like an orchestra, walking together is a good lesson in cooperation: if it's to be effective (and with walking that means fun), then adjustments must be made, deals struck, and compromises entered into.

Sometimes it might mean completely letting go of your pace in deference to the other person. When strolling with my friend Jean, who is 91, I can go no faster than she, and that's quite a letting go for a five-mile-an-hour speedster. Our occasional walks beside Strawberry Creek are full of harmony and joy, though, as we name the trees, review the garden, and listen to the quiet summer creek.

And when walking with my five-year-old friend, Ben, our route never seems to follow the straight line I'm so accustomed to when walking alone. We may veer this way for a mud puddle (to walk in it, not around it!), that way for a butterfly, and yet another way to see a water strider in a creek. Ben is a good reminder of what sauntering is all about, which is not speeding along in a one-pointed direction. His little legs, and curious mind, wouldn't allow that.

It's good to be in a situation where adaptation is required — where your ego doesn't get to do it exactly as it wants. Walking together is such a situation, and can sometimes stretch that spoiled brat of an ego to its limit.

The other day, I went up to Tilden Park with my friends Bob and Morgan for a hike along the Skyline Trail. It was funny to see the three of us strung out at one point with the fastest strider, Bob, in the lead, me in the middle, and Morgan, with her bad hip, last in line on this wide trail. This went on for awhile, but somehow, without saying anything, we eventually drew even with each other and stayed that way for the rest of the hike, with Bob chomping at the bit at times a few steps ahead. You could just see the ebbing and flowing of alone-together energy as we each tried to silently compensate for each other's presence and pace. It was a dance, choreographed by the forces of nature that require a tithing to the commonwealth. We enjoyed each other's company, not because of willful egos vying for center stage, but because of the consideration we each had for one another. If we hadn't been sensitive, we might have just as well walked alone, and given up the charade.

I still walk alone more than with others. I value it, and it nurtures me. But walking together forces a constantly changing examination of the inner self in relation to the outer environment. I cannot be the free-flying hawk, the lone wolf, the rugged individualist. My awareness of a connection to everything else is heightened. My small mind, putting me at the center of the universe, is exposed for what it is: an illusion . . . a delusion, really. In walking together, small minds often fade away, revealing one pace, one pulse, one ultimately peaceful unit not separate from the earth that brings the whole symphony together.

Piedmont

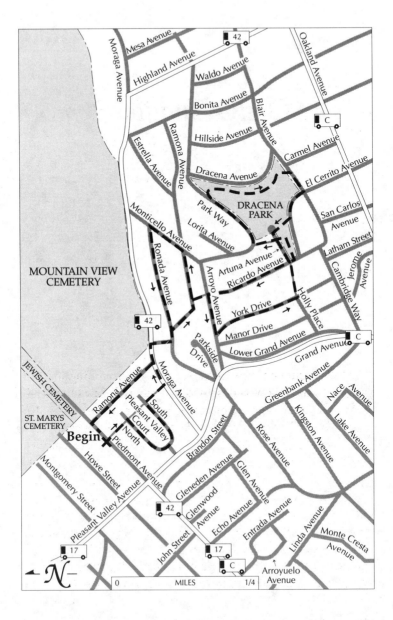

11

The Oakland/Piedmont
Way of Trees

Terrain: *easy; developed lanes and steps; broken asphalt paths*
Bus Lines: *42, 17, C (from 40th Street BART)*
Parks: *Mountain View Cemetery, Dracena, Lake Temescal*
Shops: *Piedmont Avenue*
Distance: *3 miles*
Directions: *On 580 East, take Oakland/Harrison exit, go left on Oakland, then left on MacArthur. At Piedmont, turn right and proceed to end, just past Pleasant Valley Avenue.*

The Mountain View Cemetery, near the beginning and end of this walk, was designed by Frederick Law Olmstead, the landscape architect of world renown, who also planned New York's Central Park, and opened the same year Lincoln emancipated the slaves: 1863. Olmstead was a proponent of the "City Beautiful" concept, which led to many parks, landscaped parkways, and gardens within the limits of many American cities. And Oakland and its little sibling, Piedmont, were no exception. The planting of trees was one way all communities could enhance the beauty of otherwise mundane streets, as well as provide shade and a home for birds. Olmstead led the way in the cemetery, planting many interesting species now grown to maturity, and street planners in nearby Piedmont followed suit, as this walk demonstrates.

On Piedmont Avenue, just above Pleasant Valley Avenue, find an unsigned footpath that looks like someone's back alley, next to the olive drab warehouse at #4466. It threads between that building and a cyclone fence and is opposite the Chapel of the Chimes Mortuary, designed by Julia Morgan, demonstrating her own distinctive interpretation of Beaux-Arts classicism.

The concrete path has forklift pallets on the right, along with Algerian ivy and loquat (its small, yellow, pitted fruits are quite edible when ripe), as you descend a few old wooden steps. There used to be tall Lombardy poplars along this pathway, but trees are not as sacred in Oakland today as they once were (Oakland's first mayor once advocated stiff penalties for damaging its oak trees).

At the first street, Pleasant Valley Court North, look for yucca trees decorating the house to the left, along with blackberry vines and pyracantha, a bush with small green berries that eventually turn red and cause birds who dine on them to act intoxicated (don't even think about trying them, folks). Bear right around the horseshoe court development, admiring bungalows built in the 1930s with obvious First Bay Tradition influence. The brick and shingled monuments at the entrance (junction with Pleasant Valley Avenue) are also unique, although one is completely covered by ivy. Tall California fan palms flank the entrance as well.

Continue around the horn to Pleasant Valley Court South, past the peaceful grouping of three birch trees at #4444, and take the footpath just beyond #4486 and its large Phoenix palm to the right, going up the steps to Moraga Avenue. Here, you'll find another plant connected with inebriation, the hopseed bush to the left, before you climb a few more steps and cross the speedway carefully to a few more steps on the other side.

Now turn left on the elevated sidewalk and soon see the multilayered Norfolk Island pine standing sentinel to the right at the corner. The evergreen with the drooping, melancholic branches and upright cones across the street is the deodar cedar, a native of India but used extensively as a decorative street tree throughout the Bay Area. And rounding out the street-corner arboretum is the handsome mushroom-shaped Italian stone pine across Ramona Street on the corner.

Go right on Ramona, crossing Ronada Avenue and its stand of Monterey pines on the corner. The mottled-trunk trees lining the street are the deciduous London planes, a relative of the sycamore, and a tree that when trimmed severely grows back quickly, which is good for utility maintenance crews and residents. As its name implies, the tree is favored on streets and parks throughout London.

Ramona continues to the left at the small grove of redwoods, past houses that convey simplicity, endurance, and grace. Take the footpath and steps, with an iron center rail, just past the ivy ground cover and fence, directly opposite #109. The path rises past English laurel and toyon, out to Arroyo and Ricardo avenues. Bear right on Arroyo, past oak, yucca, juniper, birch, and more pyracantha, then cross and veer left on York Drive, an open sky street with pines, palms, and a sculpted black pine, which is part of the refined garden at #12. The street trees here are mostly camphor, a relative of the Far Eastern tree that camphor is extracted from. Liquidamber has been used as a replacement tree where necessary, and there's a touch of the High Sierra with quaking aspens at #42. As for the houses, there are well-kept mission (#33 and #47) and Italianate styles (#54) along this street, as you continue to a footpath to the left, just past #68, next to the phone/utility pole. It is opposite the street Holly Place.

There are pines and acacias on this path, and the mirror plant, with its high-gloss, green leaves. Past the fence, you'll also find purple morning glories to the left and golden bamboo to the right, and at the top of the steps there are podocarpus, potato line, and pittosporum, with its small green (inedible) buds. At the top, too, is Ricardo Avenue, where you turn right to a very different street tree, the Chinese pistache, a small-leafed evergreen.

A short way on the left is an open park with a footpath up the middle. Cross and walk the path, which runs parallel to Artuna Avenue to the left and El Cerrito Avenue to the right. This is part — a small part — of Dracena Park, with a small craftsman playground and a number of tree varieties, including liquidamber, grand magnolia, spruce, Lawson cedar with its downside cones, and even sequoia. Morning glories and hydrangea add color to the array.

Exit the park to the left on the pathway, crossing Artuna to a continuation of the path, now pink concrete with a metal railing to the right of #33. Ascend the cool path, past ivy and fragrant star jasmine. Go right on Park Way at the top, past the rambling First Bay Tradition brown-shingle at #20 and a mini-Eden across the street with a recirculating stream and waterfall, along with textures and colors, all created and designed not by a professional gardener but by the owner himself. (Whether it was the garden or the hospitality of Piedmont, the owner reported to me that a badger, one of the most ferocious of wild critters, and usually found only in the Sierra wilderness, wandered into the neighborhood a couple of years ago, requiring surprised park rangers to capture it and transport it back to wherever they imagined it came from.)

Continuing up Park Way, enter Dracena Park again, this time from a higher vantage point, on a path which takes off from the sidewalk. This leads into a mixed conifer forest, on a trail that horseshoes to the right around large eucalyptus trees. It may feel like wilderness, but you're surrounded by a very quiet, genteel residential area on Dracena Avenue. There's a bench for a picnic or a cool rest on a hot day, then continue on the path which parallels Dracena Avenue.

At the stone bench, bear right, past the large oak, and bear right again, down the concrete path, into the redwood grove. At the fence, go left up the steps next to a ravine, which used to be a rock quarry but is now closed off (perhaps the badger makes its wild home in the quarry). Keep the fence beside you as evergreens give way to acacia trees, laced with honeysuckle. At Blair Avenue, stay right, as views of the Oakland skyline open. Keep bearing right at El Cerrito, down to the massive Italian stone pine and the path that leads to the right at that point. There's a city lamppost, marked #597, at this spot as well.

Walk down the steps under a canopy of California natives, such as bigleaf maple, oak, and redwood, into the park once again. Go through the park, then left on Artuna, to a right at Ricardo, with its elevated pink concrete sidewalk. There are older and tasteful stucco and brick houses on this block, as well as plum trees, and an elegant grove of deodar cedars on the corner as the street meets Arroyo. Directly across the street, take the same path as before, next to #65, out to Ramona, where you turn right. Proceed to Monticello Avenue, a street graced with cedar, sycamore, grand magnolia, and two California fan palms—the only palm native to this state, of 4,000 species worldwide—on either side of #121.

A left on Monticello brings you to Ronada Avenue, where another left takes you past London planes, exotic bird of paradise flowers, Japanese maples, Colonial Revival houses with trellises and garden fences. (The first professional gardeners in eleventh-century Italy took as their insignia the hatchet, since their main function was building trellises and arbors.)

Near the end of the street, cross and climb a few rose-colored steps, continuing on the sidewalk around the bend right on Ramona and out to busy Moraga. At the crosswalk, cross Moraga carefully, getting a closer look at the deodar cedar and the inscribed boundary wall of Mountain View Cemetery, next to a wild courtyard. The red-flowered shrub here is the wild pomegranate.

Go left on Moraga, under the cedar, then right, descending the wide-open spaces of an extension of Ramona, with its simple stucco bungalows, privet hedges, and roses, out to Piedmont Avenue and the adjacent entrance to the cemetery. It's open to the public until 5 P.M. every day and is well worth a visit to what amounts to an old, mature arboretum. There are elm (many of which are unfortunately dying of Dutch elm disease), redwood, cypress, mature liquidamber, old ginkgo, palm, leptospermum (a.k.a. Australian tea tree), along with broad bay views, pathways, Gothic-style buildings, sculptures, monuments, fountains, and graves of such notables as Bernard Maybeck, Julia Morgan, Samuel Merritt, Henry J. Kaiser, and the opulent mausoleums of millionaire's row. But the landscape alone would make the cemetery a fitting conclusion — or an excuse to return another day — to this Way of Trees.

Tree Friends

*T*rees are our friends. Again, trees are our friends. In North Berkeley, a woman proclaimed to me emphatically, "Trees are our enemies." It seems that four redwoods blocked her view of San Francisco Bay. "That's why we moved up here — for the view." End of essay. Yes, it could end here, her words reverberating through quivering groves of redwoods. But since trees can't speak for themselves — at least not in our auditory or psychic range — they might appreciate more words in their defense.

After hearing her, I hugged a tree on a walk the other day. Went right up and wrapped my arms around this massive trunk, looked up and said, unabashedly, "I love you, tree." Isn't that funny, a grown man hugging a tree? Yet if you should see me doing this on a walk, I wish you wouldn't laugh. I'm quite sensitive and so is the tree. In fact, science has shown that trees and plants and flowers are affected by human emotions. So if you laugh or snicker or make fun, that tree will feel it, and probably be hurt or afraid.

So take yourself and any children, and befriend a tree. We all need to keep some of our innocence, and trees are our reminders of innocence. A tree asks for nothing — only that it be left to grow, so it can reveal its beauty, its grace, its gentleness. Home for squirrels and birds and insects, trees seek no other meaning. Their meaning is their life. The wind comes, they move with it. The wind stops, they are still. They act not from memory or plan but from moment to moment. Fresh, new, alive. A storm comes, a branch breaks, and there is no complaint, for this is part of living, part of loving.

Yes, a tree manifests love. Clear, simple, pure love, there in front of us every day, showing us its roots, mirroring our own roots.

So if you meet someone who says they hate trees, don't waste your energy talking. Just go up to the nearest tree, in plain view, and give it a great big hug. The tree will appreciate your caring, and the antagonist might be swept up by your passion and join you.

Point Richmond

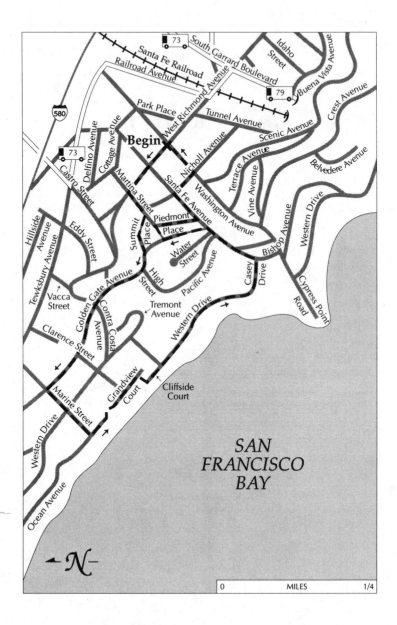

12

Point Richmond by the Bay

Terrain: *easy to moderate; developed lanes and stairways*
Bus Lines: *73, 79*
Parks: *George Miller Jr. Regional Shoreline Park, Washington School Park*
Shops: *Washington Street*
Distance: *2.7 miles*
Directions: *I-80 in Berkeley to 580 toward Richmond/San Rafael Bridge. Follow signs to Point Richmond, via Hoffman Boulevard, just before bridge.*

Point Richmond used to be a rough-and-tumble corner of Richmond—a railroad and red-light depot that even the cops stayed away from. Times have changed and the town is a calmer one, but still there are vestiges of the old order. The street map on West Richmond Avenue, at the center of town, reads "Dedicated to Bob Young and Brent Moriwaki, loved by all, shot and killed by a villain in Pt. Richmond, Jan. 5, 1989." Whether the villain's been rounded up or not, the police now patrol regularly, and the town seems safe, at least in the daytime.

Start this walk on West Richmond Avenue at Washington Avenue, cross Santa Fe Avenue, noticing the two churches to the left. The first is the Gothic-style, brown-shingled Catholic church, Our Lady of Mercy, built in 1903; and the second, at Martina Street, is the First United Methodist, a Romanesque-style, completed in 1906, just after the earthquake, which brought many more parishioners to the East Bay. Its arches, turrets, and spires were constructed with a redwood frame and faced with irregular clinker brick, manufactured at the former Richmond Pressed Brick Company, which was located on the grounds of the present George Miller Jr. Regional Park. It was built with volunteer labor at a total cost of $11,000.

At Martina, turn left, and climb to Summit Place, a footpath, with sign, to the right. This jags left until it becomes a full-fledged street — also Summit Place — which joins Golden Gate Avenue. Veer to the right, now on Golden Gate, taking the few steps down and across Contra Costa, as magnificent views of the Golden Gate and bridge open to the left. Walking under plum, bottle brush, and pine, pass Clarence Street, then go left on Marine Street at the bottom of the hill.

Now the views become inspiring, as does the apartment house to the right, with long eves and Swiss chalet balconies facing the bay. Maybeck would have loved it. Continue past Western Drive, then turn left onto Ocean Avenue at the bottom of the hill. With more Golden Gate views, go to the end, which is marked with an "End" sign, and climb the steps to the right of the sign, zigzagging to the left then right, up to a handsome mock gas lamppost. This is Grandview Court, with older First Bay Tradition houses to the left and more modern mission-styles to the right. At the crest of the hill the reason for the name of the street becomes obvious.

About half way down the hill, just past #535, take the lane to the right with the iron rail, the only railing on the block that is black wrought iron. There are more grand views as the lane becomes steps, down to Cliffside Court where you turn left. Keep descending to Western Drive, where, if you like, a dirt path gives access to a small rock beach, good for bay viewing and picnicking.

Continue on Western Drive, with its attractive mix of brown-shingled and mission-style homes, past Santa Fe Avenue, and take a left on Casey Drive. Walk up to Bishop Avenue and turn left, with views of Mt. Tam and the Richmond/San Rafael Bridge. Bear left at the top to the tricornered intersection of Bishop, Pacific Avenue, and Santa Fe Avenue. Head straight across toward the signs saying "Water Street," "Not a Through Street," and "10 MPH," finding the path to the right of the three metal posts and to the left of the guardrail. With the large brown-shingled house to the left, continue to the end of the asphalt way onto the dirt path slicing through wild fennel and coyote brush, with good views of Point Richmond village below and industrial complexes beyond.

This brings you to Golden Gate Avenue, which is more like a lane, and a concrete stairway with a metal rail, opposite #229 to the right. Descend steeply to Piedmont Place and Martina Street, and go right on Piedmont, under the large palm and beside small wood-framed cottages that once served as homes to the town's railroad workers. Turn left on Santa Fe Avenue, then a right on Nicholl Avenue — named for John Nicholl, the man who almost put Point Richmond on the international map (see page 127 for more history about Nicholl's endeavors).

The Victorian at #123 is an example of the kind of independent, owner-builder designs that you can find throughout Point Richmond. At the corner of Washington Avenue, there's a city playground and park, with palms, and antique-looking, fun equipment. Next to it, there is a church for sale (as of this writing): the Point Richmond Baptist, with its Gothic bell tower. The congregation became too small to support the building's upkeep.

A left on Washington takes you past Linsley Hall, built in 1904 as a church for an obscure denomination, which folded when its pastor left. It was originally stuccoed but is now shingled and thoroughly renovated inside and out. It can now be rented for weddings and private parties.

A bit farther is West Richmond again and the heart of the downtown district, which includes a number of buildings on the National Register of Historic Places—such as #31 Washington, built in 1901, and variously hosting a drug company, a bootery, a news agency, a clothing store, a bookstore, a cooperative arts store, and now a delicatessen; #50 Washington, a fine old brick hotel and eatery, built in 1911 in a Classical Revival style; and just about all the buildings on Park Place, particularly the Masquers Playhouse, an active community theater at #105, and the old brick fire station at #145, built in 1910. The simple one-room shack between the library and the fire station on Washington is the oldest building in town, built around 1900 for a hay, grain, and coal company, and moved from across the street, soon to be the new home of the Point Richmond History Association. The move and restoration has been a volunteer, community effort, with help from Chevron, Santa Fe Railroad, and local residents.

A final highlight is the Plaza, a small park at Washington and Park Place, built in 1988 with funds raised by community members buying small bricks with their names inscribed and inlaid in the courtyard. The Indian statue, too, was replaced a few years ago, and paid for by the community, after a long absence. The original had been knocked over by a drunk driver in 1942 (perhaps the good old days were not as good as we imagine). Each year in October, there's an Annual Indian Statue Day, staged by local businesspeople, to benefit, in part, the history association and the Masquers Theater. And the tree, giving shade and grace to the plaza, is the magnificent blue Atlas cedar.

There's a strong sense of community in Point Richmond, and in a hundred years someone, I'm sure, will be mentioning this historic courtyard in some future variation of *Hidden Walks in the Bay Area*.

The Rise & Fall & Rise of Point Richmond

A round the turn of the century, Point Richmond, a province of the city of Richmond, was similar to many Bay Area communities. There were a scattering of houses, a panoply of railroad tracks and freight trains, and no less than 34 bars lining the streets of the little village, all vying for business from the many men pouring into town to work for the railroad and a new oil drilling company. There were refugees of sorts, too, from the 1906 San Francisco earthquake, looking for a place, as people do today, that offered some security, however tentative, from having to go through another Big One.

Like Berkeley's Ocean View and Marin's Sausalito, it was a rowdy place where a bullfight was held as part of the August 1902 "Fiesta," ignoring the warnings from the SPCA and even the governor; and where Ad Wolgast out-battled "Battling" Nelson in 42 rounds, before a rain-soaked crowd at an open-air arena in February 1910.

But Point Richmond, at one time, had high hopes of world fame, which obviously didn't work out. As the story goes, one of the town's pioneers, John Nicholl, was convinced, and set out to prove, that a huge store of oil lay beneath the bedrock of the Point. He listened to C. L. Cofer, the inventer of the "Terrestrial Wave Detector," who had scanned the terrain and predicted great quantities of oil below. The device pointed to all the makings of a potential wildcat strike: large masses of blue rock, yellow and blue oil shale, and a large gas dome, now known as Nicholl Nob, which Cofer called "the hand of nature pointing to her hidden wealth and which I do register with my Terrestrial Wave Detector."

Precisely what Cofer's device consisted of was a belt of batteries strapped to his body, with a metering instrument, like a stacked deck of cards, leading the way. He took Nicholl for $50 a day, a considerable sum in those days, feeding him glowing reports of black gold lying like an ocean beneath the Point. On June 8, 1911, buoyed by Cofer's "test results," Nicholl and three other partners announced in the Richmond Independent newspaper that they'd formed a company to drill for oil. By late July, they were selling stock to finance the venture.

Soon a derrick, 82 feet high and 16 by 16 feet at the base, was built at Richmond Avenue near the railroad tracks. Nicholl called it the strongest derrick in the state. And by November, large crowds gathered, anticipating a gusher, as the drilling began. In fact they gathered so often and so closely that a fence was erected and visitors needed passes to watch.

At 60 feet, a small rock was tested by a Professor Jahnke, tagged by the newspapers as "the Wizard of Nicholl Nob," who found it to contain a small quantity of silver. He predicted a huge silver vein would be discovered farther down.

At 80 feet, drillers hit hard blue rock, and the hills shook for days as they bored through (probably rattling the nerves of those former earthquake emigres). And finally they hit it—water, that is: an artesian well and 9,000 gallons a minute caused a cave-in, while drilling stopped for a short time for repairs. Crowds grew even larger, as interest in the project swelled.

At 190 feet, they struck soft red shale, which Cofer predicted, but 250 feet of granite followed, then more water. By February 1912, they were bogged down in solid rock, averaging only 6 feet a day as the depth of the well went to 398 feet.

By April, the People's Water Company bid to buy the well, which was spewing water at the rate of 250,000 gallons a day. Nicholl hung tough, though. They were only at 500, and he vowed to go to at least 1,000 feet. They hit 20 feet of sand, a promising sign, promulgated Cofer (who presumably was still pocketing his fees), but in November 1912, after more than a year of operation, the drilling stopped at 1,232 feet.

Nicholl's dream of oil was over, and he hoped the town would buy his land for a tunnel that residents wanted for access to the bay. When the town changed the route for the tunnel instead of buying his land, Nicholl donated land around the well for the purpose of a natatorium — an indoor swimming pool — which was eventually built, using water from the well and saltwater from the bay for the pool. The original pipes have corroded, so fresh water is now piped via the local water district, but on the front lawn of The Plunge, which is what the pool came to be called, you can still see Nicholl's capped well, now locked, but filled with water and waiting for some future generation to start the pump again.

Today, people continue to swim in the popular Richmond Plunge, completed in 1925 as a community pool thanks to John Nicholl's failed oil well and C. L. Cofer's "Terrestrial Wave Detector."

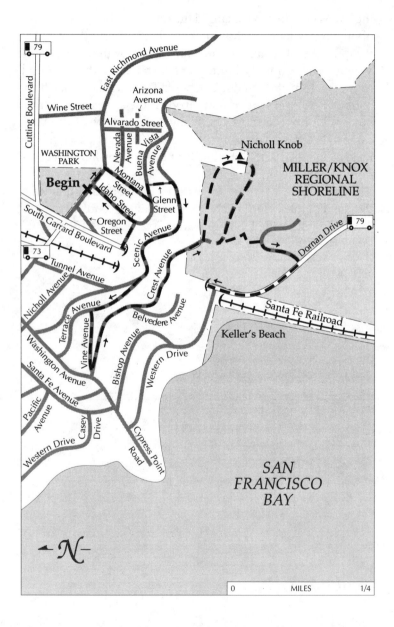

79

Cutting Boulevard

East Richmond Avenue

Wine Street

Arizona
Avenue

Alvarado Street

WASHINGTON
PARK

Nevada
Avenue

Buena Vista
Avenue

Begin

Montana
Street

Idaho Street

Glenn
Street

← Oregon
Street

Nicholl Knob

MILLER/KNOX
REGIONAL
SHORELINE

South Garrard Boulevard

73

Scenic Avenue

Crest Avenue

Dornan Drive

79

Tunnel Avenue

Nicholl Avenue

Terrace Avenue

Vine Avenue

Belvedere Avenue

Santa Fe Railroad

Washington Avenue

Bishop Avenue

Western Drive

Keller's Beach

Santa Fe Avenue

Pacific
Avenue

Casey
Drive

Western Drive

Cypress Point
Road

*SAN
FRANCISCO
BAY*

N

0   MILES   1/4

13

The Bay View Walk

Terrain: *moderate to steep; improved lanes, unimproved trails*
Special Equipment: *shoes with good traction*
Bus Lines: *73, 79*
Parks: *George Miller Jr. Regional Shoreline Park*
Shops: *Washington Street and Park Place*
Distance: *2.4 miles*
Directions: *I-80 in Berkeley to 580 toward Richmond/San Rafael
   Bridge. Follow signs to Point Richmond, via Hoffman Boulevard,
   just before bridge.*

Point Richmond was originally called East Yard when it came into being in 1900. And it was just that—a Southern Pacific railroad yard on the east side of the Potrero Hills that predates Richmond itself. The two towns joined in 1905 and experienced boom times up to and through World War II, with shipyards and auto plants drawing thousands from the South looking for work.

After the war, though, these industries, along with the white middle class, pulled out, leaving the town predominantly black and—with the lack of jobs—poor. Richmond has yet to solve many of its problems, particularly poverty and racial inequities. But East Yard—now called Point Richmond—has experienced a renaissance some would say borders on gentrification. Fortunately, many of the downtown turn-of-the-century buildings and late Victorian-era houses have been preserved.

One of the first things the railroad did was tunnel through the Potrero hills, connecting with Ferry Point, a transcontinental terminal. And this walk takes you around, up, over, and through, not the original railroad tunnel, which is still active, but an auto/pedestrian tunnel that followed.

On East Richmond Avenue, across from Washington School and Park, and its row of sycamore and pine, walk away from the tunnel, past Idaho Street to Montana Street. The small cottages in this section were originally built for railroad workers. Go right, noticing #11 with a five-bulb light fixture, brick walk and steps, and a bright garden of foxgloves, tea roses, Japanese poppies, and a bird of paradise. Passing the wild hillside to the left, approach Buena Vista with an assortment of cottages and bungalows of redwood, cedar, and arched entries, like #135 straight ahead.

Turn sharply left on Buena Vista, then go right on Glenn Street, which is actually a walkway to the right of #221. The unusual "street" starts as concrete steps then becomes a wooden-slatted boardwalk, bordered by sycamore and maple and rising to Scenic Avenue (crash site of first flight attempt—see history on page 135). Go right to "scenic" views of the oil refinery and the bay beyond. With the hillside to your left, and sporadic Monterey pine, cedar, and toyon, continue on this quiet, winding street that narrows to a single lane. Pass the shingled houses at #40 and #50, scanning the late-twentieth-century landscape of freight trains, freeways, and refineries. The wildflowers on the hill to the left balance things a bit as the signpost for Terrace Avenue and Scenic appears.

Continue straight on Terrace on a cracked sidewalk, past late Victorians to the right. Bear left on Vine Street, walking up, past acacia, eucalyptus, and buckeye, to the crest of the hill, where you make a sharp left onto Crest Avenue at the circle, opposite a sprawling Italian stone pine. The Noah's Ark-style house at

#127 bids you two by two, or three by three, or just yourself, as views of bridges, islands, and sailboats begin to open as the street bends right.

Pass Belvedere and bear left on Crest, passing the clinker-brick house and green fence to the right, and then an old railroad water storage facility that used to supply water to steam trains below. At the top of the asphalt road, take the trail that starts to the left of the fire road gate, and climb past toyon and eucalyptus, to the radio/communications towers and a spectacular 360-degree view of the San Francisco Bay Area. You are now on Nicholl Nob, where airplane history was almost made (see page 135). Look around and see if you can name all of what you see.

If it weren't so windy most of the time, it would be a good place for a full-fledged picnic beneath the grove of Monterey pine and eucalyptus, but a short snack would work out as you scan your domain. There's something about the highest place in an area that wants to be climbed, so you can now add Nicholl Nob to your life list of great peaks of the world (or at least the East Bay).

To descend, take the maintenance road to the left, winding down past the huge water tank below, and views of Mt. Tam ahead across the bay. Take a sharp left on the rough trail before reaching the gate leading to Crest and, watching your footing, go down to the trail post, bear right, then left at the next trail post. Looking over the lip of the hill, see tiny, but picturesque Keller's Beach below, with occasional bay bathers. When you get to the asphalt service road, turn right, past the old Bernardi family house and outbuildings the East Bay Regional Park District plans to eventually convert into an interpretive center, and out through the boundary gate. This open land you just walked through is all part of George Miller Jr. Regional Shoreline Park, which covers 260 acres of hills and shoreline.

Now cross Dornan Drive to the sidewalk, beside a more

landscaped part of the park (a side trip around the manicured paths and pond of the park is recommended if you have the time). Head toward the tunnel, along the quiet bay waters, getting a closer look at Keller's Beach, before crossing Western Drive and entering the pedestrian walkway through the tunnel. You can see the original railroad tunnel to the left.

Once through the tunnel, which children would probably love if billed as an adventure, cross South Garrard Boulevard to the right to Oregon Street, passing an old public shelter sign. (Before crossing you might want to explore the Richmond Municipal Natatorium, known as The Plunge, on the corner. It's a public indoor swimming pool, built in 1926, in a neoclassic style, which resulted, in part, from John Nicholl drilling for oil but striking water at the turn of the century. You can see exactly where Nicholl drilled, as the actual well is unceremoniously underneath locked metal doors on the front lawn of The Plunge. The pool continues to serve Bay Area swimmers with a variety of programs for all ages and levels.)

Now continue on Oregon, up to Idaho Street, where a left takes you close to handsome houses at #46, with its newly shingled exterior, and the Old Miller House at #25, built in 1904, with its flowery stained-glass door, gabled design, and three Swedish birches. Continuing, Idaho returns to East Richmond and the Washington School and Park, where this wild, high, and open jaunt began.

Another "What Could Have Been" in Point Richmond

Were it not for the whims of weather, Point Richmond might well have replaced Kitty Hawk in world aeronautical history. In 1900, a quiet, unassuming inventor named R. H. Botts, came to Point Richmond, intent on building a steam-powered aeroplane [sic], using his just patented and fully improved steam engine. "I understand well the difficulties encountered in aerial navigation," he announced to the world, "and the necessity of overcoming the law of gravitation is the principle one. . . . I found there was nothing to equal steam, and with that end in view, I set to work to produce an engine and boiler that would be light enough and powerful enough to answer my purpose and I have succeeded perfecting both." He then built a model airship, using lightweight aluminum for the engine, and displayed it in San Francisco and Richmond with the hopes of attracting financial backers.

By February 1902, Botts said two planes would be completed by summer, and that he would undertake an aerial expedition in June to the North Pole, to study "physical conditions of the earth's surface at its northern axis." Each airship would carry four people, supplies, and a Marconi wireless radio system. He called his company the World's Aerial Navigation Company, and shares of stock sold like hotcakes after he successfully demonstrated his engine at the railroad yard in Point Richmond on May 26.

In August, already a bit behind schedule, Botts set up his model, engine, and boiler at the Richmond Fiesta, where people took a break from viewing the illegal bullfights to gawking at the contraption. To heighten interest, Botts had fake photos made up of the flying machine cruising over Point Richmond. And it all seemed to pay off, for he raised enough money to build a workshop and hanger on Nicholl Nob, and by the end of 1903, he hauled out the finished aeroplane to an excited, if skeptical, public.

Everything was set. A kind of flying saucer–looking machine stood poised on top of Nicholl Nob, ready for takeoff and a place in history for Botts and Point Richmond. But all of a sudden, a great wind picked up and a storm blew in from the ocean, sweeping the plane off the Nob for a ignominious crash landing at the top of Glenn Avenue. Need I describe the look on Mr. Botts's face? Need I recount his anguish as he rushed to find a heap of scrap?

Botts left Point Richmond a downtrodden and defeated man, never to be heard from again. Perhaps Murphy's Law should really have been Botts's Law, for whatever could go wrong, did go wrong, and we can only hope the winds eventually blew more favorably for him.

As for Point Richmond, it remains a distinct backwater, an elbow of the city of Richmond. Its lack of fame is well intact after Botts's debacle, and present-day locals seem to like it that way.

Larkspur

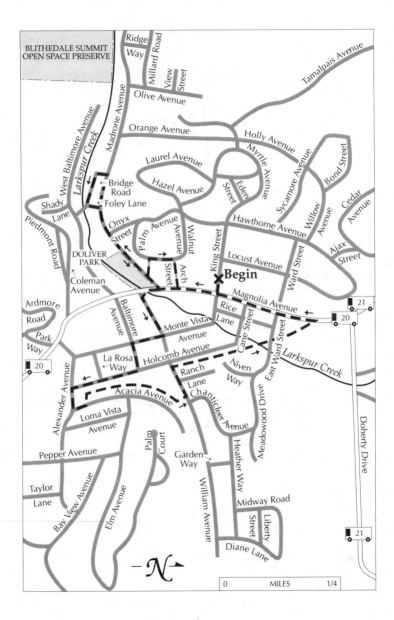

14

Of Redwoods & a
Railroad Greenbelt

Terrain: *easy to moderate; developed lanes and steps, undeveloped paths*
Bus Lines: *15, 17, 18, 47*
Parks: *Doliver Park, Piper Park*
Shops: *Magnolia Avenue, Sir Francis Drake Boulevard, Frontage Road off 101*
Distance: *3 miles*
Directions: *Follow route described in Corte Madera walk to Corte Madera's old village square. Turn right at Magnolia Avenue, off Redwood Avenue, with downtown Larkspur and King Street only a few minutes away.*

L arkspur is another Marin town that owes its existence to the railroad and the redwoods. But if you mention the town to old-time San Franciscans, they'll free associate with "The Rose Bowl," a weekly dance started in 1909 as a fund-raiser for the Larkspur Fire Department, and held among redwoods and rose trellises on Cane Street. The dance continued for many years and at its height attracted several thousand two-steppers each week from all over the Bay Area.

The other thing that drew fogbound San Franciscans to Larkspur was its sunnier climate and the possibility of summer camping among the redwoods in Madrone Canyon, then called Baltimore Canyon. The road was paved in 1914, but eco-highwaymen amazingly spared the huge redwood trees. This walk begins near this unusual street—Madrone Avenue—made narrow and cool by these ancient trees, along with old bay laurels, on and just off the street.

Start on King Street, near Magnolia Avenue, the town's main thoroughfare and one of its oldest streets. The triplet bungalows at #115, 119, and 123 were built by developer C. W. Wright around 1875 to qualify the town for a railroad station, and were among the first five homes built in town. The neat mission-style town offices, library, and fire station are across the street on Magnolia, and St. Patrick's Church, giving the flavor of a Italian village parish, completes the attractive intersection.

From King, go right on Magnolia, where another Victorian —one of the oldest in town—the Costello House, is on the corner. The house, along with mimosa, eucalyptus, live oak, bottlebrush, and Japanese maple can help you forget the traffic. Looking up, see tall stands of redwood, reminders of what this area looked like in the middle of the nineteenth century.

Now bear right on Madrone Avenue, remove your sunglasses and enter a redwood and laurel grove, lining the woodsy street. Larkspur, too, must have heard the cries of Berkeley's Hillside Club, the group that insisted on sensitive street planning that harmonizes with nature. "Bend the road, divide the lots, place the houses to accommodate them!" one of the members said of the trees. On Madrone near Magnolia, the trees are royalty.

There's a nicely placed park on the left, with playground equipment, rest rooms, water fountains, picnic tables, and Arroyo Holon, better known now as Larkspur Creek. Continue past the park, up Madrone Canyon on the right side of the street, past Onyx Street, to where the sidewalk rises well above Madrone. It feels a bit like a mountain trail here with redwoods, laurels, oaks, and even deer, at times, crossing the sidewalk.

As the walkway descends, cross Madrone at Bridge Road, continuing left past the quiet cottages of Foley Lane, then a right back onto Madrone. (Farther on Madrone, as the street winds up the canyon, there is a hidden waterfall, awaiting discovery by investigative walkers.) At Onyx, this time on the other side of Madrone, there are more redwoods and a horse chestnut tree (a relative of the Buckeye family) in the street. Now cross Madrone, before passing the park, continue on the left side of the street, with benches and sandboxes to the left, as you weave your way between the redwoods on the sidewalk.

Just before the hillside house on the left, turn sharply to the left on the concrete path leading up the hill through a grove of native trees to Palm Avenue. A right here along this narrow lane of a street, under oak and mimosa, past shingled houses and porches, takes you to a set of steps on the right, just past #9, and distinguished by an iron railing that looks like it was crafted by a plumber with leftover pipe. Walk down to Marin hillside views, tasty plums (if it's summer ripening time), mimosa, or silk, trees, and whimsical cacti gardens. The mini-mimosa forest thickens as you approach the bottom, and a lane, carpeted with seed pods, takes you the rest of the way out to Magnolia.

To the right, cross at the crosswalk next to the bus stop, and go right toward the stand of redwoods next to the Lark Creek Inn, a restored Victorian that back in earlier days when the town was filled with loggers and brakemen, was the centerpiece of the red-light district. Today, it's a fine and esteemed restaurant, pleasantly situated by the creek and redwoods.

Just past the creek, and over the bridge, bear left on the shaded dirt path leading to William Avenue. At Monte Vista Avenue, turn right past colonial-style houses, birch, laurel, palm, deodar cedar, with their drooping branches and upright cones, and a dense redwood grove, to a left on Baltimore Avenue, a palm tree promenade that formed the keystone of the Baltimore Park subdivision, one of the early housing projects that helped expand Larkspur's population.

At Holcomb Avenue, turn right, passing the very English cottage-looking house at #5 and its graceful grouping of Swedish birch trees. Proceed on Holcomb, which has no sidewalk, but is generally a quiet street with seasonal blackberries and plums for the taking, past La Rosa, with its view of Mt. Tamalpais, to the concrete bridge, which is part of Acacia Avenue. Cross the attractively designed bridge, past the Little League field, and bear left at the first street, Alexander Avenue. Neat, trim houses with cedar and pine trees are to the right, and a coppice of small trees and bushes to the left, which is where this walk goes next.

Opposite #28, there's a break in the wire fence, between two old wooden posts, as the dirt path leads down to an old railroad right-of-way, known now as the Railroad Greenbelt, and the subject of a lively fight in town to preserve it from developers and some town officials, who would like to see it become backyards. The scuttlebutt is that the development will probably happen, but the greenbelt trail will likely be saved through mitigation.

Go right on the greenbelt (a left will take you to Corte Madera), lined with blackberry and acacia, bearing right where the trail forks — the wilder side — past more silky acacia, lanky fennel, and the abandoned Northwestern Pacific Railroad's Baltimore Park substation. This was part of a railroad network that went as far north as Eureka, and south to the ferries in Sausalito. The fare from Larkspur to Eureka? Seven dollars and fifty cents, round-trip. The building, which housed automatic control equipment, has been vandalized since it was last used in the fifties, and the inside has been home to owls over the years, but it still retains its handsome mission-style features. Hopefully, mitigation will preserve it as well.

Just past the substation, take the path to the left through the gate and out onto William Avenue. After admiring the garden at #218, go left on William, past Ranch Lane, then walk right onto a continuation of the greenbelt. It's an asphalt path/bikeway next to Holcomb, marked by wooden posts and a low iron bar, and filled with acacias, oaks, blackberries, horse chestnuts, and plum trees. In fact if it's early summer and the plums are ripe, why not gather some at the side of the small bridge over lazy Larkspur Creek, near the next street crossing. Just beyond the plum trees, where the Niven family greenhouses now stand, is the site of Larkspur's first house, built by Jonathan Bickerstaff in 1852.

Now cross East Ward Street, continuing on the bike path with Mt. Tam views to the left. The California white oak, not often seen in Marin towns, can be found to the right, along with live oak, and an old train depot, with its sign and some roof shingles still intact, as of this writing. It operated up to the early fifties, mainly servicing a lumber yard where the adjacent shopping center is now located. Another old railroad building with a cathedral-like redwood door is on the left.

Passing out of this historic railroad district, (unfortunately, according to local activists who've been, so far, unsuccessful in gaining landmark status for this district, these buildings will probably be demolished), cross to the small city park straight ahead, with its young, healthy redwoods, and a plaque acknowledging this one area as the site of an ancient native American shell mound, a burial site for the Coast Miwok Indians, a wharf, a fort, and the land where Larkspur's first house was built. It was also where the Northern Pacific Coast Railroad started freight service in 1875.

Across Magnolia are a couple of Victorians that survived modernization. More historic buildings appear as you walk up Magnolia to the left, in this town that seems to care about its history. First, is the art deco movie theater, with Corte Madera Ridge as a backdrop, and then the Blue Rock Hotel, built in 1895 as the Hotel Larkspur, at the corner of Ward Street. Its name comes from the locally quarried blue rock on its face.

Continuing, pass Cane Street on the left, where the Rose Bowl held its dances, and back to King and the clean lines of the town offices and church.

By the way, the predominant street tree along Magnolia is the carob, a short, mushroom-shaped tree with long, bulbous pods, that is mentioned in the Bible. That's not why they were planted, though. In fact the public works supervisor in charge of the trees doesn't know *why* they were planted, since he told me the pods produce an obnoxious smell when stepped on, the roots are invasive, helping to crack the concrete around it, and if it was up to him . . . well, all that's another story.

Sacred Paths

The idea of holding certain paths sacred is not a new one. Holy ground, power spots, roads to Mecca, sacred pilgrimages: most of the major religions have them, American Indians had them, Thoreau had his, Annie Dillard hers, and John Muir many. One of mine is in Oakland, and though it is not as grand as Tuolumne Meadows trails, it provides a similar feeling. It acts as a screen that filters out particulate mental matter. And in the fast pace of the city, such miasma builds up quickly. Sometimes any walking will clear the channels, will slow the motion picture frames enough to regain perspective, to remember the who, what, and why of living on this planet.

The answers to these questions are not attainable to me when driving a car, or watching television, or talking a blue streak. But when out walking, or being still and quiet and taking in what's around, the answers come more easily.

At those times, humanness is more available, and what that humanness is, is the walking, is the quiet, is the taking in. Can humanness really be that simple? For socialization has taught me not to trust simplicity. Advertising hasn't and doesn't promote simplicity. There's nothing sexy about it, and it doesn't cost much, so it is devalued. There was little support for staying simple when growing up. There was spending to do, and desires to indulge in. All that took time, money, and technology. Something like walking didn't add to the Gross National Product. So I, like practically everyone, became drunk . . . with cars and TV and electric can openers and malls.

It took living in a cabin in the woods for several years to break some of the habits and mold new values. But upon returning to the Madison Avenue world, there was a need for reminders of the values that had been reshaped in the North Woods. It was nature, and places removed somewhat from the world—places not far from home, that had the spirit of the woods — that provided a nurturing of some simple spirit deep within. Some of these trails were quite close by — the waterfall off the Tamalpais Path, the trails around Cascade Falls in Mill Valley (both in the first book), the redwood grove section of "Over the Hill & Through the Woods" (in this book).

But one trail (not in either book), had something even more special — a certain quietude, a certain affinity, a certain feeling that part of my spirit was born there. It's difficult even to write about. The feeling is beyond words — is deep in the heart of the trail, communicated more through the feet. It's strange to think of the feet as a receptor, but it's really the feet that pick up what the trail gives. The mind is too enamored with the material world to hear the nuances of the trail, the fine-pitched creaks and rumblings of deep earth, the shifts in elevation, the coursing of underground water, the rise and fall of temperature as rotted matter and shadows and sun combine to cause subtle changes.

Long ago we went barefoot and our feet were more sensitive to the earth. But now technology and custom have covered our feet with all manner of "protective" layers, and have helped cut ourselves off from the body Earth, and often from our own bodies. No, this is not an op-ed piece advocating we go bare-foot all the time, but even through Vibram soles we can hear what the earth — the trail — is saying. On a spirit trail the earth speaks directly, and what is received is often a gift of forces deep within nature.

There is an intimacy that grows with walking the same trail many times, and to be intimate with anything or anyone, there is a losing of the self in it and being aware of losing that self. Then if there's a question to present to the spirit trail, there is less complexity, born from preoccupation with the self, to fog the truth from coming through. This all sounds a bit cryptic and mystical, and perhaps a spirit trail is partly that, but the clarity and simplicity of the answers is often anything but cryptic.

Yet the value and essence of a spirit trail is not to be found in the answers to questions you bring. The essence is in the communing itself. It's in the feet, in the contact with the earth. A re-connection. A re-turning of an evolutionary wheel that once knew walking as a miraculous act, much as parents know it today when their child takes that first step. Any trail, any path, then, can be a spirit trail at any moment. It's just a matter of remembering the marvel of walking on this earth.

Corte Madera

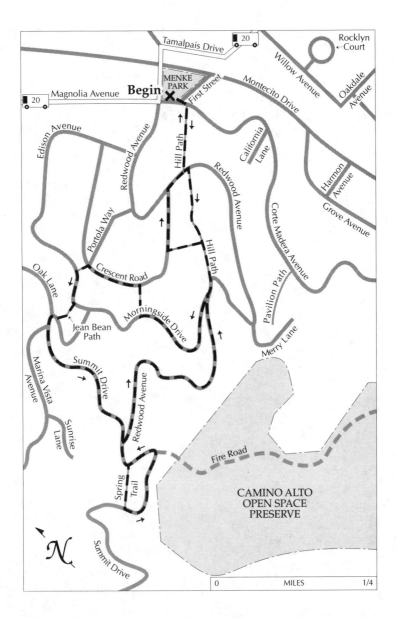

15

Christmas Tree Hill Thrills

Terrain: *steep; developed paths and steps, undeveloped sections of steps*
Bus Lines: *20, 21, 47 (Golden Gate Transit)*
Parks: *Town Park, Skunk Hollow playground*
Shops: *Tamalpais Drive, Redwood Avenue*
Distance: *2.25 miles*
Directions: *From 101, take Tamalpais Drive exit towards Corte Madera. Continue straight to junction with Redwood Avenue, then bear left on Redwood to Corte Madera Avenue on left and Magnolia Avenue (heading into Larkspur) on right.*

In 1834, all the land from Larkspur to Tiburon was owned by one man: a 29-year-old naturalized Mexican from Ireland named John Reed. He was in the lumber business and not only did he supply most of the Presidio's wood needs, but he married the commandant's daughter as well. He was perhaps Marin's first success story. But his heirs did not fare as well. For after Reed died in 1843, five years later Mexico ceded California to the United States, and the changes turned property rights upside down. Reed's family eventually agreed to a smaller claim of land, and land that went unclaimed was known as Reed Sobrantes, meaning Reed leftovers. It was this land to the west and north of Arroyo Holon, or Madrone Canyon as it's now known, in Larkspur, that formed the approximate boundaries of present-day Corte Madera.

The family eventually sold the Sobrantes to San Francisco land speculators for $2,000 in gold coin. Included in this sale was Corte Madera Ridge with its peak now known as Christmas Tree Hill, one the first sections of town to be settled. There are many mature native trees, and winding streets are connected by several convenient, and occasionally steep, footpaths and steps.

Start at manicured Menke Park, built in 1916 where the village square used to be, between Corte Madera Avenue and Montecito Drive, adjacent to First Street, and near Redwood Avenue. Obviously the town cares a great deal for this park, for willow, cypress, laurel, palm, and acacia trees are all thriving, and a peace post, decorated by local school children, is a more recent addition. Take the path, next to the bench, up the steps to First Street and Corte Madera Avenue, cross Corte Madera carefully (no crosswalk here, although you could go a short way to Redwood Avenue to the right and the crosswalk there).

Ascend the Hill Path, an unsigned lane, next to the row of plum trees, and between the cafe at #225 and the apartment building on the left. Enjoy the acacia and bay laurel as you walk up the wide concrete steps. It's not a bad place to have lunch, followed by plums and blackberries, if in season, for dessert. This emerges onto Redwood Avenue, where, slightly to the left, the Hill Path, now signed, continues up past brown-shingled houses and views of hills and ridge lands. Steps give way to a curving path, canopied with laurel, ivy, privet, mimosa, cherry, and plum, and eventually to more steps up to the Redwood Avenue and Morningside Drive intersection. Near the top of the steps, under the live oaks, admire the wood-sided sprawling house that looks like it could have been an old resort for San Franciscans when Christmas Tree Hill was just that at the turn of the century.

Now continue to the right on Morningside, the farthest street to the right, and descend this shady street, around a wooded bend with a miniforest on the right. (There is a rough right-of-way through this forest, which I contemplated leading you into, but chose to spare you the possible bramble, ticks, and sprained ankles after trying the route myself. The coppice is indicated on local maps, and I'm sure at least one of you may try it. But if anything troublesome happens, know that I recommended against it.)

Shortly after this bend in the street, and opposite #232, take the wooden steps with rail next to the gabled brown-shingled house and parking platform (another reliable landmark is the telephone pole next to the path) down steeply, past bay laurels and redwoods, to a path, then stone steps leading to Crescent, with pines and acacia shading the way.

Go left on Crescent, with plum and poplar joining the usual natives, to Portola Way, where you'll find concrete steps to the left at the crosswalk, next to a yellow fire hydrant. The Richmond/San Rafael Bridge appears on the right. (The first design of this bridge was submitted by Frank Lloyd Wright, but it was deemed to be too modern, avant-garde, and expensive. His concept involved two parallel concrete roadways, each going one way, rising gracefully in the middle. The chosen design, on the other hand, has the charm of an alligator, and the grace of a turkey, although it does get the job done.)

The path leads up sharply on broadening steps to Edison Avenue. Turn left here, past birch and pine, and just before the intersection of Morningside and Summit Drive, find the path directly to the left of #146. Turn right onto this public footpath, which first shares a driveway with the house, then continues on the red brick lane to the left of and fairly close to the house. There's no sign, but the owner of the house told me the name of the path is the Jean Bean Path, and she should know: her name is Jean Bean. Please respect her privacy with quietude.

Past the attractive house and gardens, the stepping-stone path jags right up steep steps with an iron rail, under oak, laurel, and acacia, out to Oak Lane and Summit. Bear right on Summit, and begin a careful climb—there is no sidewalk here on this fairly busy street—passing Marina Vista (which eventually goes to a trail that connects with Kentfield), up the narrow street with increasingly impressive bay views, and a great shake-shingle roof at #57, with brick chimney and rough textured stucco exterior, balconies, a morning glory–covered fence, and sentinel pines hovering above. The house looks like it could have been constructed with recycled materials, but however it was built, it all fits together and is very pleasing to see.

The street snakes upward with more broad views, and finally (it's not really that far) reaches active twin water tanks, which service the area. This is the intersection where Redwood Avenue turns sharply, and Summit continues up. Take a breather here, if you'd like, check out the hand-drawn map of the neighborhood next to the tanks, listen to the waterfall-like sound of the water, then continue on Summit about 50 feet, where the Spring Trail Hill Path begins as the street bends to the left.

It's to the left of #110, is obscurely signed, and starts as wooden steps and a path that becomes all dirt for a short stretch. Then it's an unusual wood and concrete stairway with iron rail that rises sharply, though pleasingly, through a California native forest, and a few undistinguished houses on either side. It's a workout, but the stairway is shady and cool, and the railing strong, as it veers to the right near the top, having shortcut part of Summit.

You can explore wilder trails to the right where Summit dead ends, but for this walk, go left, down (at long last!) the winding Summit, as you enjoy views of Marin open space lands and the bay. Continue on this street where it bends to the left (a fire road to the right at this point goes along the ridge to Mill Valley), back to the old water tanks.

Bear right on Redwood, continuing down Christmas Tree Hill, lined with older houses and trees, that occasionally include

California white oak and horse chestnuts, past the large brown-shingled house called "Wits End" at #653, down to Morningside and the Hill Path, with its old sign, straight ahead at the intersection. Take this path, just to the right of the utility pole, down to just past #128, with its gate signed "Thierbach," where you take the dirt path to the left, before the wooden fence starts, down to Crescent Road. Turn right on Crescent, past older, former summer homes, to a right on Redwood, where, around the bend at the crosswalk, you'll find the Hill Path to the left.

These wild fruit tree-bordered steps take you back to Corte Madera Avenue and Menke Park — the old village center, with shade and a rest on the bench near the peace pole. It's a good place to reflect upon your successful ascent of Christmas Tree Hill and part of the Reed Sobrantes.

Marin Cats

*T*hey approach slowly but quite steadily, like passenger trains coming into a station. There is no doubt in their minds. Nor are there other hindrances to get in the way of their mission. In Rome, the expression was "Veni, Vidi, Vici," I came, I saw, I conquered, but the conquering in this case is in the theater of the heart.

On the whole, Marin cats are friendly beings, not altogether fearless, for they are still cats, but more trusting than, say, Presidio Heights cats. In fact, I've never seen a cat in Presidio Heights . . . which proves the point.

The longhairs seem the most open. They preen and sit in the dappled sun to the side of footpaths, waiting for a gentle walker to come by. And that word "gentle" is important to Marin cats. You must walk with a soft step, not too fast, not too full of direction, not too decisive. Your step must convey a certain inner harmony and bare acceptance of things as they are. It must telegraph a history of kindness, perspicacity, and some attempt at realizing spiritual enlightenment. It must be cool—intimate and detached at the same time.

Once I came clippity clopping down a stairway in Mill Valley and you should have seen the cats scatter. You'd think I was Grant marching on Richmond, but worse. A few days later, though, I came down the same lane in the manner described in the last paragraph, and suddenly I was Grant coming back to Washington after Richmond. What a reception! Those cats sidled up to my leg, rolled over, hiding their heads in their paws—you know, the cute stuff that gets you to bend down and rub bellies—and followed me halfway down the steps, even beyond what they consider safe and recommended.

Even Berkeley cats are more wary than this, still retaining memory in their collective unconscious of those helicopters over Sproul Plaza, and the glow of rioting fires at People's Park.

Marin cats, on the other hand, have entered the Age of Aquarius.

As for the owners of Marin cats, I can't quite get a handle on them the way I've been able to for Berkeley cat owners. There are too many subgroups flowing in an underground river of change that seems to have the cats confused as well. In fact I shudder to think of some of them even having cats at all, imagining little Puff being dragged off to a Co-dependents Anonymous meeting, or fluffy Angelica put into a little cat pack to join Wednesday-morning master swimmers. My sense is that Marin people, much more than Berkeley people, know the value of having their cats present at all times. And it's not attachment, mind you, as they point with glowing pride at Suki Cat sitting up on her own zafu at Monday-night Buddhist meditation.

No, Marin cats are not the mere metaphors Berkeley cats are. Their lives are so integrated with their owners that they are as embroiled in such things as career development, the Mommy track, and tax-free municipal bonds as their charges. In fact, I overheard one — a cat, that is — at a pay phone in San Rafael one day talking to his broker — something about wanting salmon filet futures over the counter, which was a slight variation of a similar request the cat's owner made the day before (the basic problem was the cat copied down the wrong number, thinking his owner had called the fish market).

With all this data in mind, there *are* a few conclusions you *can* make about Marin cats. First, they all have personal computers equipped with (need I say it?) a mouse, they are all good-looking, and they are all working on (defined in cat terminology as "sleeping on") a novel. In addition, they wean their kittens at the appropriate time, getting them on a latte formula just as soon as the little consumers can paw those styrofoam cups; and they retire early (in cat years that usually comes at two), living off killings made in the past. They are also often co-dependent at birth, which usually makes them really good listeners.

Well, that's the scoop. Now you know. The truth is out. Marin will never be quite the same because I've blown the cover off its cats, revealing the ragged threads on the underside of the embroidery. So the next time you come across one of these dysfunctional felines reading Bradshaw or Bly or watching *All My Children*, pretend you don't notice. Cats have feelings, too . . . especially Marin cats.

Ross

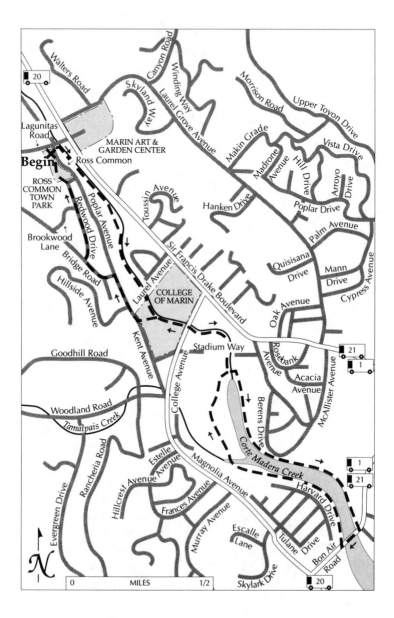

16
River Walking in Ross Valley

Terrain: *easy; developed and undeveloped lanes, bridges, and pathways*
Bus Lines: *20, 21 (Golden Gate Transit)*
Parks: *Marin Art and Garden Center, San Francisco Theological Seminary grounds*
Shops: *Sir Francis Drake Boulevard, Larkspur Landing*
Distance: *5 miles*
Directions: *From 101, take Sir Francis Drake Boulevard toward Kentfield. Turn left at the statue of the bear, in front of the town offices at Lagunitas Road.*

In early January 1982, all of downtown Ross was underwater, flooded by a raging Corte Madera Creek. Given the lazy-looking, culverted creek today, it's hard to believe it was that out of control, but a three-day rain can transform the landscape quickly. (See The Great Storm of '82 for more of what happened.)

The walk starts at the Ross Common Town Park across from the post office — a spacious, friendly park with elm, white oak, and places to both run and sit. Cross toward the post office, picking up the bike route to the right, which runs along a concrete-encased Corte Madera Creek on the left. Pass tiny Frederick S. Allen Park on the right and pine and poplar along the creekside. The traffic noise is from Sir Francis Drake

Boulevard, at one time a dirt wagon road, now the major thoroughfare along Ross Valley and beyond to West Marin.

Soon tennis courts and a wooden platform sitting area appear on the right, and then just past the parking lot of the Kentfield Rehabilitation Hospital, a wooden walkway leads back down to the creek path as you cross the Ross/Kentfield border. The creek is still culverted, but because of its shallowness and cyclone fence, some of the more exotic and skittish wading birds, like egrets and herons, occasionally feed on small fish in the slow moving creek.

As the engineering plan goes, more water begins to fill the creek at this point, and an occasional bench provides the possibility of a respite (although a better spot is just ahead). Now enter a parking lot, where you stay left near the creek, past eucalyptus on a dirt path that soon becomes paved. Wild yellow roses line the creekside as you enter the campus grounds of the College of Marin (a map helps orient you here if you'd like to explore the campus). The bike route continues along the creek with more wild roses drooping over the bank on both sides, decorating the concrete culvert.

Now cross College Avenue, and continue between the chain-link–fenced creek and ball fields. Past the last field, cross the creek over a wooden walkway and bridge, then turn right on the path along the creek. Here the restrained creek is finally liberated from the concrete, opening to its full natural banks. A small park and picnic area offers a good, albeit windy, spot to view the swooping shore birds and waterfowl, which include mallards, coots, cormorants, and the western grebe, with its black and white neck, continually diving for its dinner, or perhaps just playing.

When ready, follow the path between the now-wide creek and the small lagoon on the left, which sometimes plays host to an egret feeding in its shallow, calm waters. Soon, a wetland and bird sanctuary, with public access, come in on the left, with views of Mt. Tam opening to the right. That's Marin General Hospital off to the left on Bon Air Road.

Continue straight and cross Bon Air at the light, turning right to cross the bridge on the wider sidewalk on the other side (you could cross on the same side, but the sidewalk there is too narrow and dangerous, given the strong winds that blow across this spot). Walking on the other side gives you new views as well, with many waterfowl, gulls, and swans.

Once across, cross Bon Air carefully (no crosswalk here), then loop back up the creek on the west side on the gravel path. Residents have brightened the banks with flowers in places, and ice plants border an inlet to the left as you approach a ball field to the left. Stay straight on the dirt path around the field, bearing right onto another path leading to a small wooden bridge going over the inlet and through the cyclone gate.

The way is somewhat nondescript for the next few hundred yards, but the aim is to return to the pathway by the creek. So walk through the parking lot, past the Harry J. Pieper Field, bear right, keeping the tennis courts to your right. Bear right after you pass the courts, then left, cutting between the modern, one-story building to the left and the basketball courts to the right. At the "Do Not Enter" sign, turn right on the dirt path, ducking beneath the brush out to the grass athletic field. At the end of the large hedge, turn left, keeping to the edge of the field, going under some eucalyptus boughs to an asphalt pathway. A right on this path, adjacent to a row of old eucalyptus trees, brings you to the same bridge that you crossed earlier.

Go left to views of Bald Hill—an expanse of open space that is under pressure of development—back through the campus. Now instead of returning along the creek, walk left at Lot #11, out to Kent Avenue, where a renovated Victorian, with its welcoming garden and rose-covered gate, greets you. Turn right, passing Hillside Avenue, and take a left at Bridge Road. Traffic quiets and slows through here as the street bends to the right, passing Hermit Lane, and the older brown-shingled house at #9, with its great stone wall and entrance, and terraced garden.

At Redwood Drive, turn right, admiring the majestic redwood in the center of the street. Follow the quiet, curving street, lined with redwoods, bigleaf maple, and solid brown-shingled houses. Stay on the dirt sidewalk on the right side, as you pass dogwood, palms, and a craftsman wood and stone fence. Continue past Brookwood Lane, and the older bungalows at #24, #20, and #18, reaching the magnificent Queen Anne Victorian at #8 — the Henry Helbing House (also known locally as the Flood House, for a family that once lived there) — built in 1907, with its ornate porch, cupolas, wrought-iron fence, white stone posts, and stained glass set next to the carved front door and entranceway.

Just past the next house is a path leading into the park where this walk started. You can either circumscribe the park past a playground, athletic facilities, and benches (the Ross Elementary School is adjacent to the park), or walk across the grass and catch a Frisbee if one comes whizzing by you, or jump in a leaf pile if it's late fall. Of course, if it has been raining for a few days, you might consider seeking higher ground.

The Great Storm & Flood of '82
(1982 that is)

*I*t had been an unusually wet fall, so when the soft rain began on Sunday, January 3, 1982, and continued all night as a steady downpour, the earth was so saturated that the water had no where to go but up and out. Twelve inches of rain in 32 hours. High tides and strong winds. Four people dead. Scores injured. Over $100,000,000 in damages. Inverness cut off from the world, its water system destroyed and power gone. Petaluma inundated under seven feet of water on Payran Avenue, forcing hundreds to flee. Sausalito buried under mud slides when a steep section below the Waldo Grade gave way, forcing 300 residents of Hurricane Gulch into a Red Cross shelter—some of the women bundled in mink and chinchilla coats.

And hours before in Sausalito, Sally Baum, a 46-year-old advertising and public relations official, had returned to her house at 85 Crescent Avenue at 9:25 P.M. The road was winding, dark, and wet, and she was happy to have safely navigated the streets. At 9:35, the abovementioned mud slide carried a $500,000 house on Sausalito Boulevard down to the middle of Crescent, making "the most terrible sound," according to one nearby resident. Mrs. Baum was killed instantly as tons of mud and rock crashed into her house as the slide searched and destroyed everything in its path.

In San Anselmo, Corte Madera Creek filled San Anselmo Avenue with five feet of water, flooding every shop on the block; and downstream, in Ross, water filled the town hall basement and former jail, destroying most of its records. The town common was under three feet of water, with the level rising to the planter boxes on St. Anselm's Church on Bolinas Avenue. The Ross Grocery suffered $50,000 in damages but, with determined tenacity, was back in business in ten days. One of the young

The view from Ross Common Town Park, looking down Poplar Avenue, at the height of the Great Storm and Flood of 1982. (PHOTO COURTESY OF ED AND DON AHRENS)

men who clerks there was swept away and pulled under by the strong flood currents, coming close to drowning before being pulled to safety. On the lighter side, a volunteer, after carrying an elderly Ross resident to safety as she sat in her wicker chair, then somehow managed to steal the chair.

"There is nothing we can do! There is nothing we can do!" broadcast a panicky county communications dispatcher at one point. "We just have to let Mother Nature take its course." When it was over, Marin County, along with others in northern California, was declared a national disaster area, with help pouring in from the California Conservation Corps, the National Guard, and volunteers from as far away as Sacramento.

A year later, you could see where the trees and hillsides slid, but almost all roads were open, the Waldo Grade was buttressed with bulkheads and steel girders, tied into the bedrock, house foundations lay exposed, but the debris was cleared away, and Marin was back to normal in a physical sense. But as the *Marin*

Independent Journal put it, exactly one year later, "The mental anguish remains for many. Some still wake up in cold sweats with memories of what they saw or visions of what they think could happen to them."

And nine years later, flood control is still a major issue along Corte Madera Creek, with Ross having had to fight to save its five historic stone bridges, and contending that the county and the Army Corps of Engineers botched the design of the culvert and haven't adequately remedied it. It seems things *were* being resolved with public works supervisor Chuck Murphy on the job, but after he hit $14 million in the lottery and quit, no one had quite the same commitment to working out the problems.

Now after five years of drought, those who remember the Great Storm of '82 are fitting pontoons and Kryptonite locks to their wicker chairs, wondering if it's all building up to another monster tempest.

San Anselmo

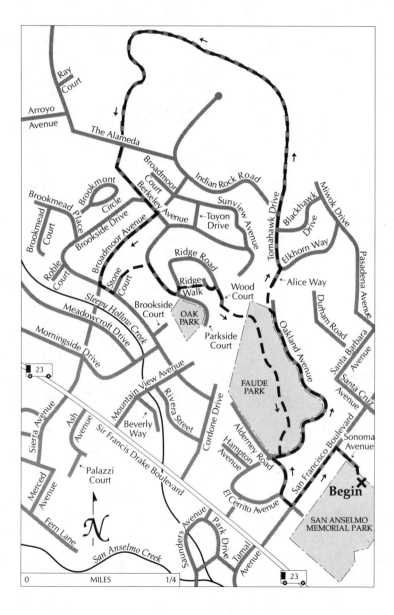

17

Wide-Open Spaces

Terrain: *easy to rough and steep; developed lanes and steps, dirt trails*
Bus Lines: *23, 25 (Golden Gate Transit)*
Parks: *Memorial, Faude, Sorich Ranch*
Shops: *Downtown San Anselmo, San Rafael, and Fairfax*
Distance: *3.5 miles*
Directions: *From 101, take Sir Francis Drake Boulevard, past five-corners intersection to a right at San Francisco Boulevard. Turn right at Sonoma Avenue into Memorial Park.*

Of Marin County's 606 square miles, almost a third is parkland of some kind. Economically, it's the wealthiest county in California, and its preserved land expands the concept of that wealth. San Anselmo, as you'll see on this walk, has done its share of preserving.

This walk starts at an historic log cabin in Memorial Park on Sonoma Avenue just off San Francisco Boulevard, which is off Sir Francis Drake Boulevard, the main connector between Fairfax, San Anselmo, Ross, Kentfield, and Larkspur. The park is public and includes a playground, picnic area, and a very active ball field. The log cabin is owned by the local American Legion post and open to the public only on Thanksgiving Day (it can also be rented for weddings and other occasions). It was built in 1934 by World War I vets (in fact, the fireplace was built by a German prisoner of war), and still used by the post and a local

Boy Scout troop. At the time of its building, it was supposedly the largest log cabin in America. Such buildings were once common in parks and state expositions but are now almost extinct (see the first book for a description of another of these log structures in the Bay Area: the Senior Men's Hall on the UC Berkeley campus).

From the park, go left onto wide San Francisco Boulevard, then right on Alderney Road. Bear right as you walk along Alderney up to Oakland Avenue. At this four-corners intersection, turn right on Oakland, with views of Mt. Tam, on the right, and Faude Park, about 30 acres of open space donated to the city in 1973, which we'll come back to for more thorough exploring later in this walk.

It's a gentle ascent up Oakland, with Scotch broom, then oak and madrone on the left, and redwood-sided houses and the hills of the Sorich Ranch open space to the right. Then just past #84, take the dirt trail to the left as it rises above the house and land signed "Now Entering Turkinney. Population 8. All creatures. Mayor." You'll see a cat crossing sign as well and a handsome redwood house and deck—apparently Turkinney's Mayoral Mansion—looking out on the hills.

The path is a short one and leads up to Alice Way and Elk Horn Way. There's an entrance and sign for the C. Fredrick Faude Park to the left, but for now, bear right up Elk Horn, using the sidewalk, with expansive views behind you. Cross Blackhawk Drive continuing straight, past Indian Rock Road. You're now on Tomahawk Drive, passing newer homes which face toward the hills of Sleepy Hollow to the north. The sidewalk winds up gently past young houses and gardens that will be antiques in a hundred years, eventually reaching a sign proclaiming a right of passage for pedestrians and equestrians on this otherwise private road, with public open space beyond.

Views open to the Richmond–San Rafael Bridge and the bay looking toward the Carquinez Straits, and Mt. Tam behind, with turkey vultures soaring above. Step through the wooden gate and begin walking up toward the water tank, but instead veer left on a wide dirt trail. There's a horse farm to the right, and ridge lands all around, as the topography of Marin comes into perspective, with its blend of open space and residential development.

Pass Snake Eye Rock—at this writing marked with a sign on the left—which, I guess, looks like a snake's eye from below. Then come to a cool grove of oak and laurel, where there used to be a sign naming the spot, Crystal Mine. I saw no crystals, but it makes a treasured resting spot on a hot day—a place to look out on Mt. Tam and smell a pinched bay leaf.

Beyond the grove is the crest of this ridge, and a sweeping 360-degree view, before the broad trail drops sharply. Stay left here for better footing as you'll avoid the loose stones and gravel. The Brookside School is below to the left, as you pass an old foundation on the way down the unmaintained road, past cedar, oak, pyracantha, and, soon, acacia and madrone. Of course, Mt. Tamalpais is an ever-present companion as it is in most of this part of Marin County. At the bottom, there's a wooden gateway with a low chain, which marks the end of an extension of Berkeley Avenue.

This leads to The Alameda, where you cross and continue on Berkeley Avenue as the street bends to the left. Pass Brookside Drive, then go right on Broadmoor Avenue, with its London planes, camphor, liquidambar, and a deodar cedar at #69 that has been shaped and trimmed, unusual for deodars and usually not tolerated by this tree. A wilder, more natural-looking cedar grows on the corner, as you turn left on Brookside Drive.

You'll find bigleaf maple and elm here, but before going too far, turn left at Stone Court, a cul-de-sac, where you head straight up the driveway/right-of-way between #10 and #17, marked on the curb, to a path and steps next to the utility pole on the right. Specifically, go up the concrete steps next to the pole, then pick up the brick steps to the immediate right. These lead to a quiet, hidden dirt path, past ivy-covered fences, and out onto Ridge Road. Now go right, under Monterey and Stone pine, eucalyptus, redwood, and juniper, to the junction of Ridge and Parkside Court, where you veer sharply left up Ridge. There's no sidewalk here, and the street is narrow, so walk with caution.

In a short while, the street bends to the right, but instead of following it, go up the driveway/right-of-way at #90 on the right, going straight to the end. Now climb a small bank, finding a dirt trail—the Ridge Walk—to the right and up, with a wood rail near the top of the trail. This shortcuts part of Ridge, and comes out farther up on this winding street. More mountain and ridge views are on the right, as you approach the intersection with Wood Court, a dead end to cars but not to walkers. Bear right on Wood, under native trees, up to but not onto the property at #17. At the turnaround there, see a set of wood steps to the left, reinforced with a small stone retaining wall.

Take these somewhat rough, snaking steps up and into Faude Park, the public open space you passed at the beginning of this walk. Follow this dirt path and more steps to where it opens near the top of the California native hillside in this primarily hikers' park. Bear right on the path with Mt. Tam straight ahead, coming to an open area, where the path continues down with the mountain now on the right. The trail levels at one point, then widens considerably and descends steeply (watch your footing on the loose rock and stone!), until it narrows under an oak grove.

At this point it winds and switchbacks more gently down the hill, using wooden railroad-tie steps, eventually down to a dirt path that takes you back to the Oakland and Alderney intersection. From here, retrace your steps back Alderney to San Francisco Boulevard, where a left takes you to Sonoma and a well-deserved rest in the park by the old log cabin.

The Hi-Line Revisited

*T*he research has continued to pour in since my first book appeared—sort of a walking "gallop" poll—and the results point to new trends in "hi" activity at places out and away from urban congestion. First, some significant racial data: very rarely does a black person venture up to a Hi-Line area—we don't know exactly why—and when it does happen, there is little "hi" contact. We've sent this raw data to our congressperson urging the creation of a President's Commission on Saying "hi" in High Places, but thus far there has been no response.

Next, we've also uncovered a stark gender-related truth: when a single man passes a single woman of similar age, there is often no "hi" exchanged, because the woman steadfastly refuses to look at the man, whom she perceives might harm her or ask her for the time as a pretext to asking her to join him for an ice-cream cone and then a date. If the man says "hi" anyway, the woman will utter a reply, sans smile, and never break her stride, which she will quicken and lengthen. There are exceptions to this (and probably marriages that have resulted from such Hi-Line encounters), but rarely is anything more than a "hi" exchanged, nor does the woman look back, which is probably wise, given California's propensity for horrific road and trailside crimes.

What showed up, too, this time is the tendency for walkers going in the same direction to ignore each other when one passes the other. This is particularly true when a lone man passes a lone woman, but also holds for most one on two, and other multiwalker configurations. In fact, at times, the woman will pause and feign an aching back, or a stone in her shoe (but never to check a map, since that would invariably draw the man to ask if he could be of assistance), or to pull out a sweater, letting the man go by, thus gaining a degree of control over what she perceives as a potentially dangerous situation.

All of these new findings have led our team to conclude that the Hi-Line is not the simple, harmonious, sanguine place we painted it last time out. There are circumstances there that would unnerve a yogi, that would drive a trucker to church, that would kill *Saturday Night Live.*

Perhaps it's a different world today and the Hi-Line is merely reflecting it. Way back in 1989, there was more friendliness. The Berlin Wall came down. Freedom invaded Eastern Europe. Russia loosened its grip and relaxed a bit. Nicaragua chose democracy, and Ortega heeded Jimmy Carter's advise and accepted defeat. Even South Africa changed its fractious apartheid course. In 1990, on the other hand, war was looming in the Middle East, the Soviet Union was breaking apart and Gorbachev with it, and economic recession was rolling along with some predicting something even worse. And the news media loved every minute of it, capitalizing on, and priming the pump of, fear.

These days, by the time we walkers reach Hi-Line places, our nerves are shot. We'd like to be friendly, smile, and say "hi," but our minds are too noisy and our hearts too hardened with thoughts of the enemy or anticipation of war or economic disasters. We'd have to stay a few days to let the filtrate of doom settle, away from radio, TV, and print waves, and allow our hearts to soften and mellow like spring snow on a southern slope.

There are signs of hope though — hard data, really. More mountain bikers, despite some of their colleagues who deface "No Biking" signs, pumping slowly up steep hills, look up and "hi" to hikers going down. And, in what might have been a skewed aberration, just the other day, a group of eight young men and women stopped their bantering and one of them delivered a clear "hi" to a lone walker passing by. The man, who happened to be this researcher, couldn't believe his ears and wasn't able to respond until several steps later. It may be a friendlier trend as people realize, despite what the media would have us believe, their inbred peacefulness and good nature.

All this heightens the need for Hi-Line protection, and so we're starting Friends of the Hi-Line, a more-than-advocacy organization that will actually be fielding political candidates. Our intent is nothing less significant than world peace, as anything else disturbs the sanctity and affability of Hi-Line places. Our mission statement comes out squarely against greed, hatred, and delusion, and is in favor of peace, love, and cooperation.

We do not expect "hi'"s all the time. People have their individual rights to pass by, eyes fixed on the ground ahead, legs churning like race horses, arms tucked up and in for speed, totally ignoring any human or other beings, as they rush to return to safe, antiseptic territory inside their cars.

What we do hope for, though, is a peaceful world where humans can begin to drop their suspicions of each other, where the first thought upon meeting is one of welcome, where a smile begins to form just about automatically, and "hi"'s spontaneously burst from both meeting parties, whatever the numbers, combinations, or permutations.

Remember, Vote Friends of the Hi-Line.

San Rafael

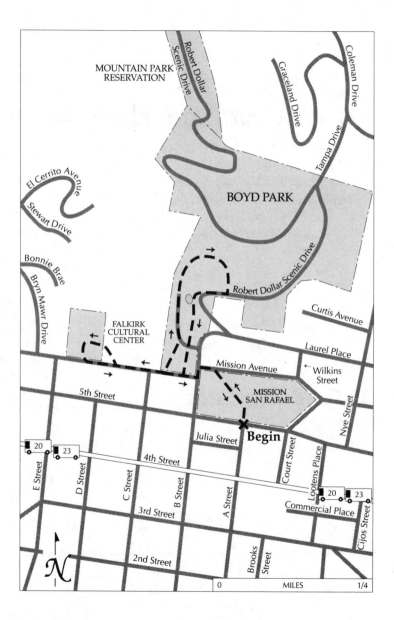

18

A Mission, Three Mansions, & a Mountain

Terrain: *easy to moderate; improved and unimproved paths, steps and trails*
Bus Lines: *1, 20, 23 (Golden Gate Transit)*
Parks: *China Camp, Angel Island, Mount Tamalpais*
Shops: *Fourth Street*
Distance: *2+ miles*
Directions: *From 101, take downtown San Rafael exit to Fifth Street. Turn left to A Street at Mission San Rafael.*

Mission San Rafael, at Fifth and A streets, where this walk begins, is a very popular tourist attraction that many first think is the original mission. It's actually a facsimile of the mission founded in 1817 by the Franciscans (see history of Mission San Rafael on page 186). The only things that survived are the bells, which now hang on the bell rack in front of the present-day church.

This walk starts at the mission on Fifth Street and A Street, and monuments facing the street commemorating those important to the mission and early Marin: Chiefs Marin and Quintin, two Indian leaders, who at first resisted the white settlers but were later baptized at the mission; John Reed, one of the first settlers in Marin; Padre Juan Amoros, who founded the mission; and 835 Native Americans buried south of Mission San Rafael Arcangel between 1817 and 1843.

Enter the courtyard—the mission and chapel were reconstructed in 1949—seeing the original bells to the right, next to the chapel, and around the corner from the gift shop. When open, the chapel offers an ongoing tape recording giving the history of the mission. On the left is the rectory, and straight ahead is the large parish church, built in 1919 and graced with Italian cypress and a couple of handsome English laurels. Irish yew, sycamore, and date and fan palms complete the courtyard arboretum.

Continue on the path between the rectory and the parish church, admiring its stained-glass window, then cut diagonally across the parking lot, finding a wooden stairway at the right rear of the bank parking lot. This leads up to Mission Avenue, where you walk left past cedar and sycamore trees, toward the ornate Stick Eastlake Victorian, which, until the Loma Prieta earthquake in October 1989, served as the headquarters of the Marin Historical Society. The house suffered structural damage, and, at this writing, is closed. It originally served as servants' quarters of the large Boyd estate.

The house is situated at the entrance to Boyd Park, but instead of entering the park here, bend to the left and continue on Mission to the right, using the crosswalk. Walking next to Boyd Park and the decorative black wrought iron and concrete fence, you get a better view of the house's gables, Victorian finery, and landscaping. Continue past the tennis court, the row of sycamores, and views of Mt. Tam and the hills surrounding the city, to a quieter entrance to the park. It's a path and steps just past the tennis court, and is marked with a plaque marking the dedication of Boyd Memorial Park in 1905.

Go right on the path, under the huge cedar and unusual bunya pine, a native of Queensland in northeast Australia, which every two years drops nine-pound seed cones from on high, presenting a real and present danger to walkers below. Look up to see if this is the year, and be aware.

Now climb a second set of steps into this friendly park with its picnic area, well-used playground, shade trees, water fountains, and rest rooms. Straight ahead, take the dirt and stone maintenance road up to a cyclone fence and observation area overlooking a fenced pond, with hyacinth, goldfish, and a waterfall. Unfortunately the fence detracts from the pond's natural beauty, but probably helps insure its survival.

Follow the dirt path to the left of the fence, up some rough steps, under a cool cover of live oaks. The path winds upward, eventually bearing right and becoming wider. It's bordered by eucalyptus as it climbs San Rafael Hill (also known as Fair Hills) above the din of Route 101. In a short while, the trail narrows, emerging into the open with views of San Rafael, the Richmond Bridge, the Bay Bridge, and Oakland on a clear day. The ubiquitous Mt. Tamalpais is off to the right, and the red-tile roofs of Mission San Rafael can be seen below.

Underneath the grove of old oak trees, take the path down through the high grass to Robert Dollar Drive (more on Captain Dollar coming up). There's no sidewalk, so walk carefully, on the right side behind the white line, a short distance to where the road bends sharply to the left. Instead of rounding the bend, go straight, under the oaks, toward the cyclone fence and goldfish pond. Descend the steps to the left to a closer look at the fenced fish, flowers, and falls. Then continue down the steps, along the culverted creek to the stone-lined path between the relatively young redwoods and alongside the creek. There are picnic tables to the left, and then two small wooden footbridges in succession, as the creek curls down past some steps, a sandbox playground, and rest rooms.

Just past the playground, find the footpath just to the right of the Victorian Boyd House. Walk slowly here, taking in the pleasures of the garden, and exit through the huge yews joining branches and gracing the gateway like a wedding bough. This brings you out to Mission Street.

Now go right, again past the tennis courts, onto a dirt sidewalk, and alongside a stone and wood-slat wall. This brings you to the stone pillars of the Elks Club. Enter the driveway, and just to the left are concrete steps leading up through privet, cedar, and English laurel to the driveway next to the Elks Club building. Go left past the front of the old Victorian mansion, which was built at the turn of the century as the main house of the Boyd estate, and cross the median strip of small acacia trees to the adjacent driveway of the Falkirk Mansion, an 11-acre tract open to the public.

Walk toward the magnificent Queen Anne–style house, with its front lawn of apple, spruce, old sequoia, bunya (watch out again, although here the staff of the mansion will place a warning sign if falling cones are imminent), and a reflecting pool. There are paths to explore behind the house, so continue around the left side, under oak and grand magnolia, to a path between the greenhouse and the small white cottage, a former servant's quarters. This leads back to another abandoned servant's house and circular courtyard.

To the left, with oak and laurel all around, duck beneath the ivy canopy and exit through the old open wood gate, picking up the stepping stone path to the left. Follow the rose-colored steps to the right down to the greenhouse, where, as of this writing, organic gardening classes are held on weekends. Go along the left side, with its juniper and mock orange providing olfactory pleasures, and continue onto the path straight ahead through the grove of tall oak, pine, and redwood. Stepping stones here lead back to the front lawn, where you can get a better look at the peaceful pool with its lily pads and small fish.

Now go up the brick steps, past Japanese maples, magnolias, and a red antique lamp, for a tour of a classic Queen Anne Victorian. There are docents who will assist you, or just wander through its 17 rooms on your own. The house was designed by Clinton Day, known for his design of the chapel at Stanford University, and was specifically adapted "to celebrate country living," as a Falkirk historical sketch points out. It was built in 1888 at a total cost of $30,000.

Day used rich woods like burled ash and oak, and a subsequent owner, Captain Robert Dollar, added tasteful wallpaper and filled the landscape with exotic trees, expansive lawns, the greenhouse, brick steps, and the pond. Dollar, owner of a steamship company and a prominent San Rafael businessman and philanthropist, was from Falkirk, Scotland, hence the name of the mansion (Falkirk and San Rafael are sister cities, by the way). In 1972, it was given national landmark status, after a battle which saved it from demolition and commercial development. The mansion now hosts the Falkirk Cultural Center, which sponsors various written, visual, and performing arts groups.

When you've had your fill, return as you came along Mission to B Street, finding the stairs in the bank parking lot, leading back to Mission San Rafael. As you enter the courtyard before returning to Fifth Street, pause and smell the lilacs at the corner of the rectory, imagining the mission bells calling the initiates to prayers in the early nineteenth century.

The Birth, Death, & Rebirth
of Mission San Rafael

As people come to Marin County now for the sunshine and open space, so too in 1817. Ravaged by white man's diseases and the chill San Francisco winter, Indian neophytes, who had converted to Christianity, were dying in alarming numbers at Mission Dolores. The change from wild to civilized life presented them with new situations they were unaccustomed to dealing with. In fact many of the dead were infants and children whose mothers lacked the knowledge this new environment required for proper care.

Responding to a letter from the mission's precept, Governor Sola thought more sun would help the ailing Indians, and, as an experiment, sent a group across the bay to a sunny hillside, overlooking the waters, but protected from the wind and fog by the range of rolling hills to the west. It worked. After a few weeks, they showed marked improvement in their health.

Soon, other missions heard of the success and sent more neophytes to San Rafael (named for Saint Raphael, the Archangel, whose name meant the "healing of God"). And in 1817, Father Gil y Taboada, the most skilled of mission padres in medical science, volunteered to serve at the new wilderness outpost.

At first, there were no plans to make it a mission, and it remained a sanitarium for five years. It became a full mission in 1822, now under the leadership of Father Juan Amoros, and by 1828 had a population of 1,140 neophytes. But Marin was not always as tranquil and mellow as it is today. In 1829, local Indians attacked the mission, out to kill Father Amoros, whom they resented for his many incursions into their land to win converts. They destroyed much of the mission and stole horses and cattle but were unable to harm the padre, for the neophytes formed a human wall around him and then whisked him away to a safe hiding place.

For the next hundred years, it was all downhill for the mission, though. After Father Amoros died in 1832, Father Jose Mercado and the Zacatecan Franciscans took over, and promptly ordered a gang of armed neophytes to attack a seemingly peaceful group of Indians who were coming to visit the mission. Twenty-one were killed, and General Mariano Vallejo, the military commandant and a neighboring land owner, saw to it that the padre was suspended and made to stand ecclesiastical trial. The court found he acted rashly, though in good faith, and only suspended him from mission work for six months. But in 1834, the mission was secularized—the first mission to be taken over by the state— and Vallejo was appointed administrator.

Vallejo then gave many of the Indians shares of property, but when it became apparent they hadn't the skills to manage the land, he recruited them to work on his own ranches for their room and board. The original adobe buildings began to disintegrate from disuse, although they did serve as quarters for Captain Frémont and his men in 1846 as they sought to secure California for the Americans.

Soon nothing remained, and the mission was abandoned in 1855. The church sold the property to a carpenter who salvaged the remaining valuable hand-hewn beams. A small parish church followed, then a large Gothic-style church, St. Raphael, was built in 1869, but burned in 1919.

Finally, a replica of the original mission was built in 1949 with funds from the Hearst Foundation. The design came from what historians considered the most accurate: sketches made by General Vallejo when he was in his 70s. The Indians are gone and a sizable town has grown up around it, but Mission San Rafael is once again at its sunny spot on a hillside away from the chilling winds and fog.

Sausalito

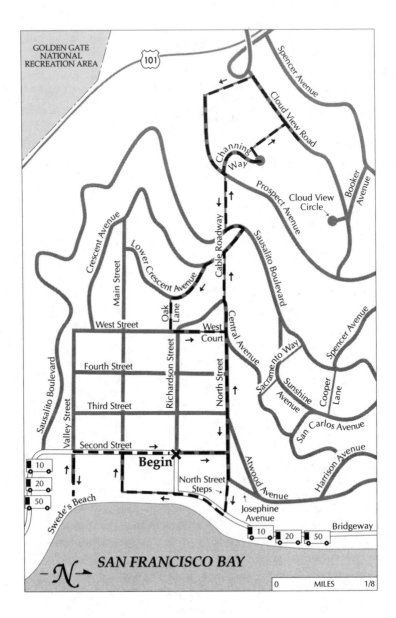

GOLDEN GATE
NATIONAL
RECREATION AREA

101

Spencer Avenue

Cloud View Road

Channing
Way

Prospect Avenue

Cloud View
Circle

Booker
Avenue

Cable Roadway

Sausalito Boulevard

Crescent Avenue

Lower Crescent Avenue

Main Street

Oak
Lane

West Street

West
Court

Richardson Street

Central Avenue

Sacramento Way

Spencer Avenue

Cooper
Lane

Fourth Street

North Street

Sunshine
Avenue

Sausalito Boulevard

Valley Street

Third Street

San Carlos Avenue

Second Street

Begin ✕

North Street
Steps

Atwood Avenue

Harrison Avenue

10

20

50

Swede's Beach

Josephine
Avenue

10   20   50

Bridgeway

SAN FRANCISCO BAY

N

0   MILES   1/8

19

Hi/Lo Sausalito

Terrain: *easy to steep; improved paths, lanes, and steps, unimproved steps and pathways*
Bus Lines: *20, 50 (Golden Gate Transit)*
Parks: *Golden Gate National Recreation Area*
Shops: *Bridgeway*
Distance: *3.3 miles*
Directions: *From 101, take Sausalito exit to Bridgeway, through center of town to Second Street and Richardson Street.*

Of all the pleasurable places in the Bay Area, Sausalito is one of the most internationally known. And because of that, the small town across the bay from San Francisco is often congested with people lining Bridgeway, queuing up with golden credit cards poised to charge.

However, there is another Sausalito — of quiet lanes and streets, hillside stairways, and turn-of-the-century architecture, all in place and waiting to be discovered and enjoyed. This walk covers a section of town from Swede's Beach to Hurricane Gulch — from the tranquil bay to a steep hillside that once slipped away in a lethal mudslide (see page 166).

At the southeast side of town on the way out toward the Golden Gate Bridge, start this walk at the intersection of Richardson and Second streets, where Bridgeway ends and merges into Second. Climb Second on the sidewalk away from the traffic to views of San Francisco, Alcatraz Island, and the Bay Bridge to the end of the street where steps continue on either side of the thickly landscaped median strip. Take either stairway, and, halfway up, cross to the other via stepping stones under pittosporum and oak. A barking dog, who sometimes surprises, seems to be well-fenced.

This leads to North Street, where you carefully go left using sidewalks when possible, under a sprawling Italian stone pine. Pass Atwood Avenue, then cross Third Street, skirting South View Park, with a lawn, tennis, basketball, and benches with great views — the entire park, though, is a bit too run-down for a town with the wealth of Sausalito (it's the 45th wealthiest suburb in America).

Cross Fourth Street, using a short sidewalk on the right. Then bear left at Central Avenue, with the Waldo Tunnel and Grade above and a five-globe lamppost at #50 that T. A. Edison would've loved. To the left of #35, where Central horseshoes left, ascend the old stone steps, staying left if a decision arises. This is the Cable Roadway, marked with a sign — a favorite path of mine that also appears in *Hidden Walks in the Bay Area*.

It's a steep climb through a forest of cedar, horse chestnut, acacia, bay laurel, live oak, on a semblance of stone, dirt, and finally wooden steps near the top, with a welcome rail to pull you up to Crescent Avenue. Walk carefully to the right — no sidewalk here — to Sausalito Boulevard, where you turn left. As you turn, notice the concrete steps with green pipe rail to the right, next to the #575 mailbox. (Yes, this is a public way.) Take the steps and go left on the dirt path, running parallel and above the street. This leads to a wooden walkway and rail, then concrete steps to the right under a coast live oak tree.

At the top is a driveway/right-of-way — this is still the Cable Roadway — leading up to Prospect Avenue. Bear left then an immediate right onto Channing Way, where your assault on the summit continues, winding to the right, past a brown-shingled newer home, with fanciful whalelike cantilevers. The house design may have been Maybeck-inspired, since he used such carvings in his houses as a way of honoring his father, who was a woodcarver.

At the top of this cul-de-sac, bear left up another drive-way/right-of-way, past the Dachshund-crossing sign (careful you don't trip over one!) to the wood steps and rail to the right, just before the end of the driveway and opposite #8. These public steps lead up to the water tanks and pumping station, where you continue on a pathway/driveway out to Cloud View Road.

We'll soon come back to this spot, but for now a short jag to the right leads to added attractions. Just past the mission hacienda at #80, see the huge wooden sculpture of Saint Francis at the corner of Cloud View and a private road on the left. He's holding an animal, of course, and is well hidden, despite his size, in a grove of live oak.

A bit farther on the right is one of the most secluded, and scenic, playgrounds in the Bay Area. Enter the weathered gate and trellis to toddler swings, a sliding board, sand, carousel horses, and a bench, dedicated to David Campbell Criley, 1975–1985. Around you are yucca, acacia, spruce, Japanese maple, and an old brown-shingled (and locked) community house, with (unlocked) brick paths and courtyard.

When you're finished with park pleasures, head back up Cloud View, paying homage again to Saint Francis, under Monterey pine, cypress, and white and stone pine to the street's end. Pass through the white guard rails — that's the 101 freeway ahead of you — and turn left on the dirt path. Across the freeway, trails lead to Wolfback Ridge and the Marin Headlands beyond.

Now descend the long steep stairway straight ahead, passing acacia, eucalyptus, oak, and cypress to Prospect. A left takes you past Channing Way, then go right on Cable Roadway once again. With the bay and Angel Island ahead, find the stairway at the bottom and even better views of popular Angel Island (a great state park with spectacular trails and views, accessible by ferry from Tiburon). Zigzag down to Sausalito Boulevard, jagging left then making an immediate right onto Crescent. The bay views are wide and open here, but take care since there are no sidewalks. Pass the Cable Roadway, then bear left onto Lower Crescent and in a short distance take the steep steps to the left, just past #42, under the live oak tree and next to a utility pole. This is Oak Lane, of concrete and dirt and organized steps, with good views along the way, down to West Street.

To the left is West Court, where you climb the steps at the end, past modest cottages, modern mansions, and wind chimes that give voice to bay breezes, up to Central. Turn right, then bear right on North Street, taking in a whole city and half the bay at a glance. Pass Third Street, then Atwood, using a sidewalk when available. Pass the same steps you came up at Second, and find steps to the right under a stone pine, where the street bends to the left. These are the North Street Steps, with iron rail.

It's an elegant descent past the gardens of Casa Sonada at #201, and, about halfway down, a stone bench to the right offers good views and a place to rest. Continue down, under cool acacias, to busy Bridgeway. With the small park on your right, cross Bridgeway at any point here (no crosswalk, but a median strip and an unobstructed view provide safety) to the sidewalk by the bay.

Walk right, with nothing but water between you and San Francisco. In a short distance, take the boardwalk to the left and proceed past two older homes, with decks and bayside lawns, which seem a bit odd to see, and a restaurant, then head around the bend on the walkway onto Main Street and out to busy Second Street.

For the final gem of this walk, go left one block to Valley Street, turn left, and, at the end, descend the wooden steps to perhaps the most hidden public beach of them all: Swede's Beach. A plaque, set into a stone cairn, shows the beach is dedicated to the memory of Fire Captain Ralph K. "Swede" Pedersen. There are a stone bench, some sand and quiet waters, and open views of Angel Island and Belvedere with Tiburon beyond. Oak and laurel give some shade, so just about all of your beach and bay needs could be met at Swede's Beach, albeit on a small scale.

Now return to Second Street and go right to the crosswalk at Main, then cross and go right, staying on Second. At Richardson, the loop is complete. You have probably now experienced more of Sausalito's topography than most of its natives, and probably all of its tourists.

Falling

The night before my friend and I fell off a cliff at Point Reyes National Seashore, I was telling a fellow Christmas party reveler that walking has never caused me any problems. On the contrary, I told him, walking has always provided a clarity of mind that helped me solve problems and navigate through some pretty murky waters at times.

Perhaps it's a mistake to tempt fate like that for the following day, we set out — it was our first date — on an eight-mile jaunt to a lovely place called Alamere Falls — a wonderland where water falls pell-mell from a high cliff onto the beach. And for seven of those miles, all was well. We talked and walked and sat and picnicked and laughed and even kissed and hugged.

But in the eighth mile we saw firsthand proof of the Buddha's admonition that life can change as quick as the swish of a horse's tail. We started back from the falls late — around four — with darkness gradually, almost imperceptibly, overtaking the light. We were both feeling buoyant from the falls, the ocean, the sounds, the pelicans, the warm California winter sun. I had a flashlight in my fanny pack but was liking the sensing of the trail with my feet.

"You know, I used to cross-country ski in New Hampshire at night without a light, and I did my best skiing then," I told her, remembering the exhilarating feeling of plummeting down an incline using my feet, my gut, my heart, but not my eyes, to reach the bottom. At those times, I had no fear and never skied better. "It *is* getting pretty dark, though. Would you like a light?"

"No," she answered. "I kind of like this feeling of walking in the dark." She must have been a little scared, I thought. But I let it go and continued talking animatedly about dark New Hampshire nights.

"I had to walk about a mile through the woods to my place there and . . ." The next word I do not remember for it never came out. Instead, I dropped from the seemingly solid trail into an abyss that ended about 15 feet down, although at the time I couldn't tell how far down I was.

In the next instant, something came tumbling down on top of me—a rock I thought from the crumbling, unstable cliff bank. But a rock does not groan. It was my date, and she was below me a few feet, having tried to grab me as I fell and getting too close herself to the gravelly edge. Her wrist was broken, and I mean broken, now shaped like a lightening bolt. My ankle was sore, but I intuitively knew it was intact.

In one false step—that was actually quite real—life had changed and would never be quite the same. There would now be memory—memory of falling, memory of losing ground, memory of the danger of walking at night near a cliff without a light. The fall itself took less than a second, but within that time, the seed of a lifetime was planted. I would more respect the night now. I would be more careful of knowing the terrain at any given point. I would anticipate more: not out of fear but out of the memory of experience. I would pay more attention to the act of walking itself instead of being intoxicated with talk, leaving walking to fend for itself. Walking needs attention. Walking needs care. Walking needs love.

I would remember, too, falling—a state human beings are unaccustomed to. It has been a long time since we swung from tree to tree, falling in between until we could grab another vine. It has been a long time since we jumped off a cliff into a deep lagoon of clear blue water. We try, at all cost, to avoid falling. We insure ourselves against it. We safeguard our bathrooms. We shovel and chisel and salt our sidewalks to make sure it doesn't happen. We equate falling with disaster: the Bay Bridge and the Cypress structure of the Nimitz Freeway after the big quake in the Bay Area. Entire movies are based on the fear and anticipation of falling. The word evokes images of broken bones, emergency wards, casts, and sometimes death.

But when I fell, I was not afraid. If a stop-action camera had captured me during the fall, it would not have picked up a fearful face. I think instead my face must have been quite serene, somehow comfortable with falling, enjoying the feeling of space around me with nothing solid to inhibit or constrict. It wasn't the falling that presented the problem as much as the ground I hit when the fall stopped, and the ground I looked up at as I pondered our predicament.

Later, it made me wonder if death is like falling and birth is the ground we eventually hit. I've always been afraid of the idea of death as well as the idea of falling, but the feeling of falling itself was enlivening. There really was no problem when I was airborne. Could death, too, be exhilarating—a kind of falling with no surrounding ground? Could birth be the ground that suddenly, rudely, intrudes on the ecstatic falling of death?

After the fall, I hauled myself out of the dark abyss, now using the previously shunned flashlight. Then I hoisted my injured new friend out, pulling her arm so straight that it cured a trick elbow of hers in the process. Her wrist was obviously fractured, although I valiantly tried to wish it otherwise. Thankfully, she was not in much pain. My ankle was sore, but we both could trek the remaining mile back to the trailhead. We were lucky, I guessed. The drop to the ocean near that point was at least 200 feet.

Yet during that second in the air, from the trail to the ledge below, maybe I *was* in a state of death, in a state of falling, and without the mind to deny it, or explain it, or worry about it, or lament it, I was free. I was at peace.

No, I don't recommend taking a dive off a cliff. But maybe the mind doesn't always have to have a ground, a reason for everything, a need for tangible reassurance. Maybe I can let myself fly a little more, take more risks, and even fall. It's a scary thought, but somehow exciting and life-affirming.

Of course these musings are all well and good, but when my

friend Bob asked me the day after the fall what lesson was the universe trying to teach me, what came to mind was 1) use a light when hiking at night, and 2), on a first date, go to a movie.

Alameda

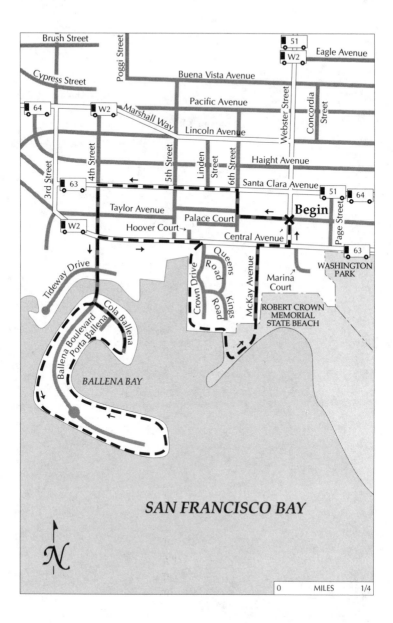

20
Alameda by the Bay

Terrain: *easy; developed and undeveloped footpaths*
Bus Lines: W-2, 51
Parks: *Washington, Crown Beach, Shoreline Drive, Crab Cove*
Shops: *Webster Street, Otis Drive*
Distance: *4.3 miles*
Directions: *From Oakland, take Webster Street Tube to Webster in Alameda. Continue straight to Taylor Street, the street before Central Street where Webster ends. Caution: Obey the posted speed limits. Alameda police are known for very strict enforcement.*

I n some ways, Alameda seems a bit out of time. With its naval base, all-night diners, and lack of skyscraper office buildings, it has the feel of a sleepy late forties town, still awakening to a seemingly more complicated world beyond its connecting tunnels and bridges. Real-estate brochures in the 1870s, when railroads and ferries were expanding, promoted Alameda's "Healthful climate, perfect sewage, finely macadamized streets, park-like drives, charming homes, pure artesian well water, and pleasant, convenient rail and ferry service." It's still a pleasant place to live and visit, but add noisy navy jet and transport planes, traffic jams through the tunnels linking it with Oakland, and a crowded shoreline that has been extended through much too much fill. Still, if you want to recapture the flavor of an earlier America, go to Tillie's Diner around midnight.

Alameda's first houses were built at the eastern end, and its first commercial district at the western side, closer to the bay, which is where this walk begins. At the end of Webster Street, start on Taylor Avenue, with the Queen Anne turret on the corner. Walk north on Taylor to Sixth Street and the Mediterranean lines, pink stucco, red-tile roof, and bell tower of St. Barnabas Catholic Church. Go right on Sixth, past #1458 with its stylish craftsman features to a left on Santa Clara Avenue, with a number of Victorian beauties clustered among more contemporary housing. The ornate Queen Anne Victorian made use of stock ornamental designs supplied by local wood shops, and could be applied to large houses for the wealthy as well as smaller cottages. Paint, too, was a way to brighten the exterior and was accessible to the commoner as the "painted ladies" (as such Victorians are often called) at #548, 540, 452, and 454 attest. The Queen Anne cottage at #529 even uses Islamic decor to further distinguish it.

Turn left at Fourth Street, admiring the Queen Anne/Stick Eastlake Victorian on the corner, built in 1885. At the corner with Taylor is a classic, larger Queen Anne house, with its tall palm, stained glass, and unusual fake carriage house front to the left. Cross the wide and busy Central Avenue, entering the Ballena Bay complex, a large, fairly tasteful development built in the late sixties, when the town allowed its borders to be increased, and the San Francisco Bay decreased with an extensive fill operation.

The bay may have suffered, but walkers benefit from this man-made peninsula. Passing the entrance to the complex, glance in and see the fountain and some of the gardens. The grounds are not open to the public, but prospective, or even mildly potential, residents can walk around after getting permission from the office. It's worth the time and effort, as paths wind through minilagoons, lush vegetation, wading ducks, fountains, and landscaped waterfalls.

Whether you've taken the detour or not, continue across Tidewater Drive, crossing the bridge over the lagoon. This becomes Ballena Boulevard on the other side. Pass Cola Ballena, then cross Ballena Boulevard at the crosswalk, turning right alongside large bottlebrush trees. Just past Porta Ballena, the sign reads "Ballena Isle Marina and Ballena Bay Yacht Harbor," where you cross over to the public shore access, marked to the right.

This skirts the bay via a dirt path to the left with views of naval base battleships, the San Francisco skyline, and the hills south of San Francisco. The winds are often stiff here, as sea birds and pleasure boats lean into it. Views open all the way to the long, low San Mateo Bridge. The path soon becomes sandy as you approach a short chain fence and plaza, with anchors and the mast of an old schooner that once plied bay waters, perhaps with vegetables from the small farms of what is now Bay Farm Island.

Follow the paved road to the right, past a burned-out former French restaurant, taking the dirt path, lined with ice plants and fennel (neither of which is a California native), to the right of the fenced area along the shore, out to the end of the point. (This may soon be the site of a large hotel development, which will still retain this public access shoreline you're currently walking on, though probably in a paved form.) Across the way is Crown Beach, former site of Neptune Beach, a very popular amusement park in the early twentieth century, and Crab Cove (we'll be there shortly), with a row of tall fan palms behind.

Keep the water to your right as a marina comes into view, picking up an asphalt roadway again. With swaying masts and city skyline ahead, pass yachts with names like *Sail La Vie*, *Wind Song*, *Toad*, and *Livin Life*. (Collecting yacht names might be a fun game if you have children along.)

Pass through the yellow gate, staying on the walkway past the Ballena Bay Executive Center, complete with a delicatessen on the left, and a relaxing promenade straight ahead, offering marina views, benches, and a restaurant featuring outdoor seating and looking out onto the marina—definitely one of the nicest restaurant views around. At the end of the walkway, there's a quiet bench, where you go left, carefully, through the parking area, crossing to the sidewalk to the left as soon as possible. This street is Cola Ballena, which crosses Porta Ballena, and then Ballena Boulevard.

Now retrace your steps to the right, back across the bridge, this time going right at Central Avenue. It's a busy, wide street, the attractive large redwood house at #510 being one of the few treasures of its past. But you're not on it long, needing only to go past Fifth Street to Hoover Court, where just beyond, take the path to the right, marked as a public shore at Crown Drive.

The foot and bike path winds down to the right, through an automatic gate that is open from dawn to dusk. (If you get trapped inside after hours, no need to panic: just push the button on the post next to the gate, and it will open.) This is another hidden promenade, along a serene inlet, lined with ice plants, willows, poplars, benches, and wind chimes, giving a voice to the bay wind, which is often strong here. There are houses and a broad, private lawn to the left with gracious willows, and then another automatic gate inviting you into Crab Cove, a public park and regional shoreline, part of the East Bay Regional Park District.

Follow the paved path, leading to the Crab Cove Marine Reserve, a recreation and education wrapped in one package . . . and, at low tide, fully accessible to those in wheelchairs. There's an excellent visitors/interpretive center (open between early March and the end of November) a bit farther on this path, so check for guided tours, low-tide times, and plan on spending some time learning about bay ecology and Alameda history.

Crab Cove became a regional park in the mid-sixties and

offers paths, ponds, picnic areas, lawns, and the cove itself, which resulted from fill used in the expansion of Neptune Beach in the 1920s and residential development after World War II. It is, in fact, home to crabs, specifically the green shore crab and, to a lesser extent, the purple and sand-lined shore crabs. The park also hosts an annual summer sand castle–building contest, producing some of the finest sand sculpture and architecture in the West, if not the entire country.

When you've had your fill, take McKay Avenue next to the visitors center and across from the federal center complex. At Central, turn right, but not before taking a slight detour to the left. It's Neptune Court, just to the left on Central and the only structure, now an apartment building, that remains from the old Neptune Beach complex. Peek into the courtyard at the fountain and ornate scroll work.

Now continue right on Central to Webster Street and another Alameda landmark: Croll's Bar and Grill, with its rare mansard roof, on the southeastern corner, and in business since 1883. It's the town's oldest continuous commercial establishment and, at one time, rented rooms to turn-of-the-century boxers such as Gentleman Jim Corbett, training across the street at Neptune Beach. Inside, you'll find wood paneling and beveled mirrors that date back to the bar's origins, as well as memorabilia of the boxers who stayed there. East on Webster returns you to Taylor, where the art deco Nation's Restaurant across the street keeps you back in time—a good place to be in Alameda by the Bay.

A Matter of Life and Death

I was 38 when I first noticed the birth of a leaf—the effect of growing up in a row-house East Coast city. Before, there was winter with bare branches, and then suddenly a quick spring, followed by a long summer with trees adorned in fully mature leaves. For almost half a lifetime, one of the premier shows of nature escaped my attention.

The birth of a flower blossom from its small bud was more obvious and eye-catching. But with the leaf's bud, the expectations were so muted, they were not worthy of much attention: an ordinary green, sort of fully developed leaf curled up in fetal position, one day appearing in fullness. But a leaf has a flower, too—a very delicate flower with all the accessories.

This discovery came because of a carless spring one year—a going on foot for all business and errands. Walking each day brought a slowing down and a consequent seeing what had been in front of my olfactory apparatus for all those years. At first, though, it was unbelievable. It must have been what early human beings felt like when they realized that making love led to babies. Before that awareness, as theorized by prehistorical novelist Jean Auel, they didn't link the two events. Since becoming aware of the birth of leaves, I have never let another spring go by without spending time with deciduous trees.

Another event that went unnoticed was the actual moment a leaf left a tree in its fall to the ground at the end of the growing season. There had been millions of leaves falling, but never the isolation in my awareness of any one leaf leaving the twig to which it clung. Why this was so important had to do with missing another of nature's most significant events—the moment of the death of a leaf.

So the watching began, and lasted a long time, focusing intently on one particular leaf, not knowing how long it would take. An hour went by, then a second hour—a trancelike hour concentrating on that leaf. There were even times when the distinction between leaf and self blurred. Scary stuff — losing boundaries — but the seeing provided the anchor to reality.

Finally, without fanfare, it fell, swirling to the ground. I rose slowly, never losing sight of it, and picked it up. It was a maple leaf, crinkled and brown and drained of life. It was dead, but somehow it was a part of the part of me that sees — the part that understands what it sees not in words but in feelings. It was the part that remained alive, for in nature, its death would lead to life.

These two events — the birth and death of a leaf — may seem of little importance in relation to that which the news media would have us believe is important. The birth and death of leaves are rarely reported on, and only a search of obscure poetry will reveal anything on the subject. But contemplating the life cycle of leaves has offered a perspective on life not usually received from newspapers, books, or even an entire college education. It offers a perspective that this life, in this moment, is connected to all life that has been, all life now, and all life that is to come.

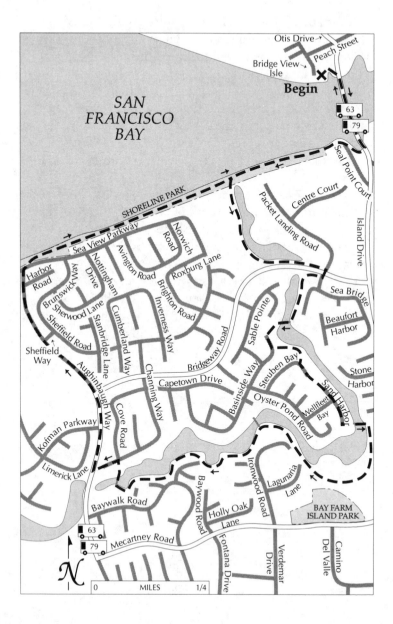

21

Water, Water, Everywhere: Bay Farm Island

Terrain: *easy; improved and unimproved paths, lanes, and bridges*
Bus Line: *79*
Parks: *Shoreline, Crown Beach, Crab Cove, Lydecker*
Shops: *Shopping centers on Mecartney Road and Otis Drive*
Distance: *4.5 miles*
Directions: *From Oakland, take Webster Street Tube to Webster in Alameda. Continue straight to Central Street where Webster ends. Turn left and take first right onto Westline Drive, then left on Otis Drive. Continue to trailhead at Peach Street and Bridge View Isle, just before Bay Farm Island Bridge. Caution: Obey the posted speed limits. Alameda police are known for strict enforcement.*

At one time, from the turn of the century to the mid-sixties, Bay Farm Island was a scant spit of land, consisting of several small farms, supplying produce, by ferry, to San Francisco. But as people poured into the Bay Area after World War II, someone had the idea that another Bay Bridge was needed, so a massive fill operation was started on the island to support the East Bay side of the new proposed bridge. It was the last time the shrinking bay would be filled in such proportion. About a thousand acres were bulldozed into existence. The land is still there, but obviously the bridge never got off the ground.

Developers, of course, looked longingly at this choice and vacant bay-front parcel, and by 1978, the first homes were built, with the battle cry being "Live, work, and play in Harbor Bay," as the community was called. To date, 2,400 homes have been built, with 600 more planned, a sizable business park is being developed, there's a tastefully designed shopping area, and a wonderful network of lagoons, foot and bike paths, playgrounds, small beaches, and a shoreline park that weaves the whole community together in a very agreeable fashion, as this long but level walk demonstrates.

The walk starts just off Otis Drive, near Peach Street and Bridge View Isle, near the Bay Farm Island Bridge. From the dirt lot by the water, take the path up to this drawbridge and cross with the racing traffic safely separated from you behind the fence, with views of San Francisco, the bay, Mt. Tamalpais to the right, and the Oakland/San Leandro hills to the left. At the other end is a U.S. flagpole and the Alameda Vietnam War veterans memorial, where you turn right, down the dirt path to a sidewalk along the water, passing a fishing pier/utility cable bridge on the right and tennis courts, bordered by Italian stone pines, to the left.

As you pass the bridge, enter Shoreline Park on the right via the asphalt walk/bikeway. There's a row of cypress, pine, and privet on your left, and then a wooden walkway with benches on the right between the very public dwindling marsh and wetlands of the bay and the very private Harbor Bay Club swimming pool. The wood gives way to dirt as you continue with expansive Bay Area views. But in a short way, the path is blocked by a fenced pumping station, that looks like an electrical generator. This pump is part of a flood control system that regulates the flow of fresh and salt water in and out of the lagoon system on Bay Farm Island. And to the left of the station is the start of one of the lagoons and its walkways.

So bear left on the path just before the willow trees, keeping the lagoon to your left. It's a quieter world here of small willows, colorful gardens across the water, ducks, and some of the least skittish egrets and great blue herons I've ever seen. Around the bend, busy Bridgeway appears with a cool grove of poplar, willow, and plum trees by the lagoon. Continue to the crosswalk at Packet Landing Road, past a redwood bus stop and a large quaking aspen, and cross Bridgeway to the right. Turn right on the other side and very shortly see a path to the left, again following an extension of the lagoon. Proceed under mature pines and poplars, past lazy weeping willows and a lanky Lombardy poplar just before the sturdy wooden bridge.

Cross the Walt Jacobs Bridge (named for the volunteer of the year in 1986 by the Harbor Bay Isle Owners Association), then bear left past one of the well-placed and skillfully designed playgrounds (each with a unique jungle gym arrangement) on the Island, coming out to the end of a cul-de-sac, where you bear left again to a small beach and playground by the lagoon (the lagoons are quite shallow, but the water is suitable for bathing and wading, especially for young children). Just past this area, cross the street ahead and go straight to the end of a cul-de-sac to another innovative playground park. Wind under the pine grove near the lagoon and past a small beach, coming out to the end of a street called Sand Harbor. Pass Wellfleet Bay and bear left at the end of this street, finding, to the left of #85, a playground, park, and an elevated wooden bridge, next to a large quaking aspen.

Cross the lagoon, perhaps pausing to take in this Southern drawl of a spot. Pick up the path to the right, and enter a well-thought-out shopping center built at water's edge. Keep bearing right through the area, which includes an inviting bookstore, restaurants, a deli, a cafe, and even a church and synagogue. The lagoon path continues past the last building, where Monterey pines line the way just before another elevated bridge. This time, though, pass the bridge, rounding a bend to the right, past another of those small beaches. The houses are a Mediterranean style as you come to a horseshoe bend with a private swimming pool to the left.

Just beyond this point, cross the sturdy bridge, bordered by willow and poplar, to the right, past the small sitting area to the right, and straight out to Channing Way. Turn left here, with new brown-shingled houses on either side, to a short path leading to Aughinbaugh Way. Go right and stay on this street, admiring its varied street trees, which make this otherwise boring and sometimes busy street bearable. They include the knobby trunk London plane, which is related to the sycamore, the mushroom-shaped Italian stone pine, poplar, plum, and the yellow paloverde, with its long seed pods (most seed pods found in nature, by the way, are not edible, and even garden peas, if eaten in too large quantities, will sometimes cause gastrointestinal difficulties), near Sheffield. The large vacant lot across the street will eventually host a school.

Aughinbaugh feels like it'll never end, but in shorter time than you might think, it takes you back to the bay. After crossing Sheffield Way and Harbor Road, follow the red brick crosswalk at Sea View Parkway, and enter Shoreline Park, where a picnic area greets you. Bear right, picking up the path adjacent to the water. The houses along here are brown-shingled, and classified as Seaside style, according to the developer. But a more interesting view may be of the bay and Alameda to the north, and the Oakland Hills and the Coliseum to the east. This is near the bird sanctuary on the other side, so you may see some interesting migratory ducks here too.

Now come to the same bay water-pumping station, and you've made a full loop. You've walked about four miles to this point, so pat yourself on the back (if you're still standing). Just a bit farther on the same path as before, pass the classic design of the Harbor Bay Clubhouse on the right, the wooden walkway by the bay, the pines next to the tennis courts, the Vietnam memorial, and back over the Bay Farm Island bridge. Notice the small marina of the historic Aeolian Yacht Club to the right as you hear the echo of cars over the metal grate of the drawbridge. Across the lagoon, you're now back to where this four-and-a-half-mile, thousand-acre, aquatic journey began.

The Walking Song

Words & Music by Stephen Altschuler

Maybe on the prai - rie   Where the golden eagle   flies

And while you're moving your feet along why don't you use your ears and eyes.

The Walking Song

Well it don't make no difference
where you live and breathe
And it don't make no difference
your opinions or beliefs
And it don't make no difference
what trail you tread upon.

Chorus
Just set your feet a-walkin'
and take your spirit along.

Verse
Well it don't make no difference
if it's sun or rain.
And it don't make no difference
if you're angry or in pain.
Just get out of your buggy
and start to sing this song.

Chorus
Just set your feet a-walkin'
and take your spirit along.

Bridge
Well maybe by the ocean
on a cliff way high above.
Maybe by yourself
or with someone you love.
Maybe on the prairie
where the golden eagle flies.
And while you're moving your feet along
why don't you use your ears and eyes.

Verse
It don't make no difference
if you're young or old.
And it don't make no difference
if you're shy or if you're bold.
'Cause nature is a social club
where everyone belongs.
Chorus
(Just set your feet a-walkin' . . .)

Well maybe on the East Coast,
or maybe on the West.
Maybe Minnesota,
or a Dixieland address.
Close your eyes and point your finger,
you never will go wrong.
Chorus

Well it don't make no difference
if you're a woman or a man.
And it don't make no difference
if you have no map or plan.
Just pick up on the rhythm
beat your chest like old King Kong.
Chorus

Supplemental Reading

David Gebhard, Eric Sandweiss, and Robert Winter. *The Guide to Architecture in San Francisco and Northern California*. Salt Lake City: Gibbs Smith, Publisher/Peregrine Smith Books, 1985.

Kenneth H. Cardwell. *Bernard Maybeck: Artisan, Architect, Artist*. Salt Lake City: Peregrine Smith, Inc., 1977.

Sara Holmes Boutelle. *Julia Morgan, Architect*. New York: Abbeville Press, 1988.

Jacomena Maybeck. *Maybeck: The Family View*. Berkeley: Berkeley Architectural Heritage Association, 1980.

Elna Bakker. *An Island Called California*. Berkeley: University of California Press, 1971.

Adah Bakalinsky. *Stairway Walks in San Francisco*. San Francisco: Lexicos, 1984.

About the Author

Stephen Altschuler is a writer, a teacher of creative non-fiction, and a walker who leads walking tours based on his books. If you'd like more information about his walks and/or writing seminars, write to him at P.O. Box 20985, Oakland, California 94611.